MW00594309

© 2012 Freedom Life Christian Center

The statements contained in this book are substantially true. Some names and minor details have been changed or withheld to protect people, situations and organizations from accusation or incrimination.

Unless otherwise noted, all Bible quotations are taken from the New International Version, Copyright 1973, 1984, 1987 by International Bible Society.

As noted within the text, Bible quotations are also taken from the New Living Translation, Copyright 1996, 2004, 2007 by Tyndale House Foundation.

ISBN: 978-1478338390

My Back Story

True Stories of Freedom and Life

As Told To
Jeannette Scott

To the passionate and dedicated people of
Freedom Life Christian Center
who have given their time, talent and treasure
during the past 40 years to fulfill the Great Commission.
Countless lives have been changed because of you!

-Pastor Sam Masteller

To my husband, Bob Scott, for his sacrificial
love and patience with the author.
To my children, Craig Scott and Becky Scott
the best two reasons to
live my own story forward, no turning back.
And to the courageous friends who
expose their souls on these pages
that others may find freedom and life.

- Jeannette Scott

Contents

Introduction

The longer you live, the more you realize there is always a story behind the story — a back story, if you will. Things are not usually as they first appear. As you read the stories on the pages of this book, you will meet incredible people that I know very well and love very much. Each of them has overcome tremendous challenges in their lives.

They were drowning in guilt and despair, but found the secret to swimming in calmer waters. Their stories remind us that we all have a back story that doesn't have to haunt us anymore. These real people bear their souls on the following pages in hope that you will experience the same freedom and life they have found.

Sam Masteller
Lead Pastor
Freedom Life Christian Center

Love's Last Words

Jake Wood's Back Story

My dilated pupils surveyed my companions as we sat in a circle on the living room floor. At times I'd catch their possessed eyes rolling back and forth while their demonic laughter ascended in my ears.

"Jake, dude, don't you know where you are?" one guy laughed.

They were liars, all of them, taunting me with assurances that I was still in my friend's Denver home. But I knew better.

I was in hell.

I hurried — almost floated — from my surreal surroundings into the silent winter darkness outside. I crunched across four inches of snow to stand alone in the salted street and scan my environment. There had to be someone, anyone, who would verify what I knew to be true.

Two cars cruised slowly toward me and I flailed my arms to stop them. Surely the driver would confirm I was in Satan's lair! The cars came too close so I stepped out of the way and watched them roll by into oblivion. There were no drivers.

Oh no, I realized in this nightmarish place.

Hell wasn't white-hot flames and the stench of sulphur.

It was a lonely permatrip on earth, void of all contact with another soul, except these laughing, evil-eyed imposters. My friends were demons all along, and they succeeded in their mission to imprison me here forever.

I had thought there was more time ...

I was born to a loving, church-going Denver family in January 1978. My mother had several types of jobs over the years, and my father was a printer. Many in our close extended family were pastors of one kind or another.

From as far back as I can remember I embraced the Christian life. Church attendance wasn't a ritual in our family, but a reflection of genuine faith played out in everyday life. Our closest relationships outside of family were with people we knew from church.

My brother Jon was born a year after me, and Jessica followed a year behind him. Money was tight, but we kids never knew it. My siblings, our friends and I had the run of the neighborhood and imaginations to occupy us. We played church and preached sermons to each other . We played starting lineup for the Broncos with pajamas wadded in our shirts for shoulder pads. We dug in the dirt and raced our bikes up and down the street. Our adventures only ended when the streetlights came on and our fathers called us home.

Every so often Dad would disappear for a day, or two ... or a week. Grandpa, Grandma and Mom toted my siblings and me along to search hotel rooms and hospitals for him. By the time I was a preteen, I understood that Dad was a drinker. No one hid it, but no one made drama of it. It was simply the rhythm of our otherwise perfect family life.

Dad was prone to excruciating headaches and the booze gave him some relief. We witnessed his pain at times, but he did his drinking out of sight.

One day, when I was about 11, I heard someone at the front door. I opened it to find my subdued father sitting on the front step and without a word, he gathered himself and stumbled into the house. I had never seen him drunk before. In fact, I'd never seen *anyone* drunk before. This wasn't my dad. Something was off.

Only once did I overhear some vague discussion of divorce and it shook me up. I didn't know anyone who was divorced, and certainly not in my family. Not cousins, aunts, uncles or family friends. We would be the black sheep.

We're not that family! I thought as I lay sobbing on my bed. *We still love Dad. We want him here. This can't happen because we're the perfect family!*

Dad and Mom stayed together and Dad made the rounds in and out of different treatment programs such as Teen Challenge. Mom joined him at a marriage rehab where Dad had a spiritual awakening of sorts and came home a new man. He didn't drink or disappear anymore, but the severe migraines continued.

I was in sixth grade at the time and a few months after Dad's transformation, I shuffled around the house, anxious for him to get home from work with my allowance. I didn't want to be late for my standing Friday night roller skating date with my girlfriend. Time ticked away and soon it would be too late to go. *Not a good time to go on a bender, Dad*, I thought.

My girlfriend's mom came to the rescue and drove us to the rink to meet our friends.

At the rink, a disco ball swirled colored spots on the maple floor and walls as we wheeled to the beat of predictable skate music.

"That girl's all right with me, yeah. She's a super freak, super freak," the Rick James skate classic blared. "She's super-freaky, yow."

Snack bar lines grew when the Hokie Pokie interrupted "All Skate" time. Those without girls hit the arcade for *Super Mario Bros., Exterminator* and *Pac Man* during "Couples' Skates." Meanwhile, other boys fumbled to skate backward to 80s ballads like Journey's "Open Arms," as their Girlfriends of the Hour hung on their necks. I was not in the arcade that night.

My girlfriend's mother pulled up to my house to drop me off and Mom bolted out of the door to greet us, breathless.

"I ... I ... just got a call. Just got a call," she was frazzled, distracted. "There's been an accident. Dad was in an accident and they won't tell me his status. We've got to go to the hospital, right now."

Here we go again, I sighed as my girlfriend's mother drove my family to the hospital. We'd collected Dad more than a few times after accidents during benders. *And it seemed like he was doing so well this time.*

On this night, things were different. When we got to the waiting room, my grandparents were already there. Our pastor was there. Friends from church and other family members trickled in. Doctors in scrubs came in and out of the room like yo-yos to talk with my mother and pastor. Then one of them summoned Mom to go with him.

When she finally returned, she stepped aside to whisper with my pastor and burst into tears. Then she gathered my brother, sister and me and we sat down in the waiting room chairs. "I'm so sorry kids," she said. "Dad died."

All physical sensation washed out of my body like the tide. My thoughts shut down, unable to process what was happening. My sudden mental fog would last for weeks.

Jon was hysterical.

"I want to see him," he urged with tears.

"No, honey, not now. I'm so sorry, not now," Mom and my grandparents consoled him softly.

But he only got louder. "Every other time I got to see him. Why can't I see him?!" he bawled.

Later, we would understand that Mom was being kind. The accident was brutal and the viewing would be a better place to say goodbye.

Dad was on his way home on the freeway with my allowance when a passing motorist watched him slump over the steering wheel. His car veered left, jumped the median and hit an opposing truck head-on.

He wasn't drunk.

He had a cerebral hemorrhage while driving. Later, it was explained to me that while Dad was fighting merciless headaches all those years, blood was leaking into his brain.

Grandma took Jon, Jessica and me outside for some fresh air. She didn't talk, which was good. As we sat on a bench, I stared at the starry sky and watched a few birds fly in and out of a tree. *I just saw him this morning, and now he's gone.*

We usually took the bus to school, but we were running late that morning so Dad dropped us off. Jon, Jessica and I hopped out of the car, swung our backpacks over our shoulders and started toward the door to make first bell.

"Stop. You guys gotta stop," Dad said through the open car window. We paused and turned around.

"You know I love you," he said deliberately, looking each one of us in the eye.

"Yeah, yeah, Dad. Love you, too. We gotta go," we said and hurried on.

They were good last words to have.

Seedling trees lined the drive and walks of the cemetery where we buried Dad. I sat on a cushioned folding chair in the designated family section as our pastor said a few words over Dad's flower-covered casket. A well-known musician from Nashville and a pastor from South Carolina joined a crowd of mourners at the graveside to pay their respects.

When our pastor finished the service, the mourners single-filed past our family, offering hugs and the promise of prayer. One relative put her hand on my shoulder and said, "You'll have to be the man of the house now, Jake."

When the last of the mourners trickled away, I thought, *This is the last time I'm going to see my dad.*

As they lowered Dad's casket into the ground, my heart went with it.

I always accomplished what I set my mind to do and that didn't stop with good grades. My dad's death triggered a determination to get close to God.

I really connected with the youth pastor, who let me join the youth group early because of losing my dad. He became a mentor to me at the time and I really needed that. His wife had contracted AIDS from a blood transfusion, and she passed away that year. A number of people at church were uncomfortable with her illness so the church let him go. His termination caused uproar and some people left the church.

In less than a year, I'd lost my father, my youth pastor and the stability of my church family.

Soon afterward, Mom and Grandma took my siblings and me on a summer-long road trip to visit family in Kentucky and South Carolina.

I had always looked up to my uncle who was then a youth pastor in Kentucky, so I was eager to visit him. As our family sat beside him in the pew one Sunday, the pastor closed his sermon about following God's calling in life with a challenge.

"Everyone bow your head and close your eyes," he said. "Let God speak to your heart right now ..." his voice trailed off as images in my mind grabbed my attention.

Behind my closed eyes stood an army of young men and women dressed like ancient Roman soldiers. I was training them for war on a battlefield just like the one in the film *Braveheart*, (which had not been produced yet). I was teaching them how to defend against and how to attack their enemy.

The pastor's prayer was answered. I knew God had just spoken to my heart and called me to youth ministry.

"Please come forward if you would like us to pray with you," the pastor invited.

He didn't have to ask me twice.

"You'll have to be the man of the house now, Jake," my relative's words rung in my mind. I became protective of my younger brother and sister and even my mom. I locked the doors at night, made sure my siblings did their homework and helped mom with the house and yard. Mom told me I shouldn't feel responsible to "be the man," but I was determined.

I was 13 and just completing eighth grade when we finally got a new youth pastor, Dan, after a series of interim ones. During my freshman year, my mother started dating him. She'd been on only a few dates in the two years since Dad died. It wasn't awkward that she was dating — enough time passed that I could accept it. It was just a little weird at first because Dan was my youth pastor.

Though I didn't mind, and my siblings didn't seem to mind, there were people in the church who did mind. Mostly they were uncomfortable that Dan was ten years younger than my mom. Rather than fight a losing battle, he resigned and we joined a different church.

I was 16 when they married.

"I now pronounce you man and wife," the pastor declared with great enthusiasm. Cheers went up and the weight of manhood slid from my shoulders. *I can be a kid again,* I sighed.

"How ya doin', Jake," my youth pastor asked a few months later.

"Good, man."

"Really? You don't seem as into God as you were when you first came here," he said.

"Yeah, right now I just want to float," I replied. "I want to do nothing. I want to float down the river."

Until that time, I'd been a good kid but wound tight with the self-imposed responsibilities of manhood. Now, I could relax. Let loose. Try out some of the things my peers were doing.

About sophomore year, I added partying to that list and, as with everything else I did, I went all out. I drank a few times, but the image of Dad on the steps and Mom's warnings that "It could be in your blood so you better not start," kept me from frequent or heavy drinking.

But when a friend from school and youth group got some weed, I was eager to smoke it. We made a pipe out of a soda can and got high before school. Now this was the stuff for me!

Gradually, I transitioned to a new set of friends and learned where to get pot. I quit youth group because I didn't want to be a hypocrite.

As I dove head first into the party scene, my new friends and I experimented with acid (LSD). The first time I tripped was in the park with two female friends. The park morphed into a mammoth size loaf of bread and we were inside it! The girls and I pressed through the sides to get out and then went to the movies to watch *Natural Born Killer.* Boy did that movie mess with my hallucinating mind!

Tripping led to adventures. My friends and I would drop acid and seek profound revelation from imagined sources of wisdom. We went for a walk to find a bush because the bush had answers. We hiked in the mountains to search for some transcendent spiritual experience with a boulder or a tree.

One day, as we each dropped a couple hits of acid, a friend said, "Yeah, I'll never do powders," referring to cocaine, meth and heroin.

"Yeah, that s*** is messed up," I agreed. It was the general consensus that we would *never* do those because they were reserved for *real* drug addicts.

Yet, I'd already established my own addictive affair with hallucinogens. Acid was my drug of choice and I tripped about 150 times in a year and a half, sometimes taking as many as eight doses. I dropped them in my eyes for fast absorption and sometimes tripped for three days straight.

My academics suffered and I dropped out of school in my junior year.

Mom and Dan knew something was up and continually confronted me.

"What are you on?" Mom would demand.

"Nothing! Just get off my case would you?!" I'd say. They'd try to catch me in the act, but never could.

I smoked cigarettes and pot, so I needed lighters but they kept disappearing. Later, I learned my mom and Dan accumulated a drawer-full from confiscating them!

About a year into the party scene, my "never" became my "usual." I snorted coke once in a while, and got into meth as much as LSD.

"Yeah, man, I don't know how those junkies can shoot up," I said at a friends house, holding one nostril shut and snorting a line off the coffee table with a rolled up dollar bill. "I could *never* do that."

"I know, that's messed up," one of my companions agreed. "Especially when they share needles, man. That's just wrong."

Even addicts have a code of ethics. Twisted, but still a code of right, wrong and more wrong. Mainliners (intravenous drug users) were at the bottom of the barrel.

The progression of my full-blown addiction continued and when I was 17, I dropped two hits of acid with some friends one night.

Even with as much acid as I had done to this point, this was the first time I had a bad trip. My mind and vision swayed in and out of reality.

I'm dying. I just know this is it. I'm dying.

Then, *No, I'm just tripping really hard and I need to ask someone if we're okay.*

Then again, *I'm dying. This is real. I walked away from God and now I'm dying and going to hell! I know it!*

My dilated pupils surveyed my companions as we sat in a circle on the living room floor. At times I'd catch their possessed eyes rolling back and forth while their demonic laughter ascended in my ears.

"Hey we're okay right? I mean, I'm just trippin' hard. I'm not dying, right?"

"Jake, dude, don't you know where you are?" one guy laughed. Others joined in.

They were liars, all of them, taunting me with assurances that I was still in my friend's Denver home. By now, I knew better.

I was in hell.

I hurried — almost floated — from my surreal surroundings into the silent winter darkness outside. I crunched across four inches of snow to stand alone in the salted street and scan my environment. There had to be someone, anyone, who would verify what I knew to be true.

The quiet block seemed abandoned, as if aliens had transported all life forms across the Milky Way. I simply had no idea that it was four o'clock in the morning, when most of the town slept.

I tried not to slip as I ran up the snow-covered sidewalk in search of signs of life. A guy was delivering newspapers to a business.

"Hey, dude, me and my friends, we took a bunch of acid. I'm tripping hard and I need to go to a hospital. Can you help me?"

"Jibber jabber, wah wah wah," everything out of his mouth was mumbled and garbled. Finally, I made out a few words.

"Call 9-1-1," he said, handing me a fist full of quarters. "With this phone right here." A payphone magically appeared and my savior left to continue his route.

With all the effort I could muster, I focused to get some quarters in the slot. Then I dialed, struggling to press the moving keys correctly.

9-1-1.

The phone rang and rang and rang. Eventually, I hung up and stood in the street.

Two cars cruised slowly toward me and I flailed my arms to stop them. Surely the driver would confirm I was in Satan's lair! The cars came too close so I stepped out of the way and watched them roll by into oblivion. There were no drivers.

Oh no, I realized in this nightmarish place.

Hell wasn't white-hot flames and the stench of sulphur.

It was a lonely permatrip on earth, void of all contact with another soul, except these laughing, evil-eyed imposters. My friends were demons all along, and they succeeded in their mission to imprison me here forever.

I always thought there was more time. After all, God had called me into the ministry! Surely he wouldn't let me die without my final surrender to follow him! This was just my wild stage. After all, shouldn't I have a dramatic life story like other Christians?

It was too late to change my fate. There's no way out of eternity and I'd inadvertently made my choice of where to spend it.

"God, give me one more chance!" I cried anyway as I dropped to my knees, frigid snow soaking through my jeans.

It wasn't my first foxhole prayer. Yet here I was, pleading again. "I'll change my life! I'll serve you in ministry!" I sobbed.

Two friends from the house found me. They lifted me off my knees and practically carried me back to the house.

"Let go of me, you demons!" I shouted. "You're just pulling me deeper into hell!"

"Jake, it's alright. You're gonna be fine. Dude, you're gonna wake up," one of them said.

They got me to the house where I slept off my altered state.

When I woke up, one of the guys passed me a bowl and I took a hit. I knew something had to change, but how?

I continued to smoke pot and do meth. Friends and I were breaking into houses — up to four a day — and pawning our loot to pay for our habit. We sold fake acid to people at raves (underground parties with techno or psychedelic music, dancing and drugs). I was involved with influential and dangerous dealers. In spite of wanting to be close to God again, my life was spinning further out of control with no way out.

A few weeks after my bad trip, my 22-year-old cousin invited me on a road trip to South Carolina to visit his dad (my uncle), who was a senior pastor.

Maybe if I get away from this scene and see family, I'll get it together, I thought.

My uncle was one of the people I respected most, and Mom had told him that my life was out of control. The night before I headed back home, he invited me to come live with him.

"Thanks. We'll see," I told him and left it at that.

By the time I got home, I knew what I had to do. This was an open door — a way out of my cycle of insanity. If I stayed on my current path, I was on the fast track for jail, a mental institution from bad dope, or death. I was most afraid of death. My bad trip still haunted me. Though my experience was chemically induced, my possible fate was real. Hell was void of hope with no way out and I'd had a taste of it. But here and now, I could still find God and find my way to heaven.

I gotta take this offer, I thought. *If I don't take this, I know where I'm going.*

For several months, I joined my uncle and his family at Sunday services. I wanted to turn my life around, but still wasn't committed to this Christian thing like I was when I was younger. I only attended church out of respect for my uncle.

I also wasn't into seeing a Christian play in Augusta with his family and church members but I wanted to be agreeable. *The Masterpiece: A Toy Maker's Dream* was a drama about a toymaker who chose to be punished in the place of the rogue figurine he created and loved.

Having grown up in church, I understood the play was an allegory for the Bible's account of how Jesus volunteered to be beaten and nailed mercilessly to a cross to pay for my own rebellion. From childhood, I'd been told that if I believed this, and asked God to forgive me, my crimes against God and others would be pardoned. God would make me into a totally new person and be my loving Father.

Because of my calling to youth ministry, I always thought God would do something dramatic to intervene, like part the skies in a vision. On this day, there was no powerful message, no emotional plea. I wasn't writhing in sorrow or bursting with joy. But God was here and I was here and this average moment seemed as good a time as any to make things right with him.

You gotta stop. You know I love you.

The soft streetlights were on, lighting the way toward home. My romp around the neighborhood was over.

"If you would like to ask God for forgiveness and let him change you," the host said from the microphone. "Please stand."

I rose to my feet, tearless and committed.

It was no light decision and my companions knew it. I was all in, ready to leave my old life behind and take marching orders from my Father, God.

Like a toddler who constantly asks, "Why?" I hounded my uncle daily with a barrage of questions. I didn't want to learn religion; I just wanted to soak up God like a dry garden takes rain. This was the perfect environment to do it, too. I was at church for every service and every activity. I became a student leader in youth group.

A year later, I went to visit my family in Denver. My youth pastor advised me not to visit the people and places of my old life, but I was a fireball and wanted to help everyone find Jesus and experience God's love like I did. Surely, they'd hear me out.

My first stop was the hell house where I had a bad trip. The same people were inside partying.

"Hey, Jake. Good to see ya, man," my buddy who lived there said.

"Yeah, where you been? I heard you got religious or something," another guy asked.

We talked for a while and they mocked me as one of them tightened a cord around his bicep and searched for a vein in the crook of his arm. He poked the needle in and slowly plunged the syringe. He passed the same needle for the next guy and leaned back to ride the rush.

The next "never" was now the "usual" here.

Oh God. This could have been me.

"Hey, take a hit from this, dude," one of them said, passing a bowl.

"Naw, man, I'm done with that stuff. What are you guys doing shooting up, man? It's gonna kill you," I said. "God has a better plan for your life than this."

"If you don't f***ing hit this, I'll beat your face in," another old friend threatened.

Their taunts continued. "Get you're a** over here and drink this."

An outsider looking in, I finally saw the insanity of it all. I left that house for the last time, grateful that God made a way out. I prayed he would do the same for them, and I never looked back.

As I drove to my parents' house, I thought of the story Jesus told in the Bible in Luke Chapter 15. In the story, a son took his inheritance from his father and left home to spend it on the party life. He ended up destitute and was forced to become a servant for a pig farmer. Starving, he considered eating some of the pods that he fed the pigs. The guy had hit bottom.

He went back to his father, hoping he would take him back as a hired servant. Verses 20-24 (NLT) continue the story.

"... his father saw him coming. Filled with love and compassion, he ran to his son, embraced him, and kissed him. His son said to him, 'Father, I have sinned against both heaven and you, and I am no longer worthy of being called your son.' But his father said ... we must celebrate with a feast, for this son of mine was dead and has now returned to life."

How would my mom react when she saw me? I'd put her through so much. I'd broken her heart to the point that she begged God to get a hold of me no matter what tragedy was necessary. She had every right to slam the door on my face or at the very least give me the cold shoulder. I didn't deserve to be her son.

I entered the house with tears and wet cheeks.

"I'm so sorry, Mom," I burst out crying. In an instant she was hugging me tight and sobbing, too. "I love you, Jake. I'm so glad you're home."

I had returned to high school in South Carolina and excelled in my studies. After graduation, I went to Christ for the Nations Institute in Dallas to study practical ministry for two years.

I found my zone as one of the leaders at a campus youth group for the teens of CFNI students. I'd been doing that about a year when a new CFNI student from Oregon joined our ministry team.

Kim thought I was cocky and I thought she was fun to be around. I had a girlfriend and she had a boyfriend and we shared a circle of friends. After a while, both of our romantic relationships ended and our ex-significant others got married!

As Kim and I served side-by-side in the youth ministry, it seemed we were always in sync. We began to wonder, *Could we be right for each other?* We weren't jumping into anything though because we both were done with the dating scene. The next person we each dated had to be a good candidate for marriage.

One day we were sitting in my car, discussing our futures when it occurred to us that our ministry callings were a perfect fit.

I wanted to be a youth pastor, a front man. She wanted to be behind the scenes as mama to the youth. I wanted to be a good father. She wanted to be Mother of the Year. Her strengths complemented my weaknesses. My strengths made up for hers. Besides that, she was beautiful inside and out!

We started dating in 1998 and a little more than a year later, we married in Kim's hometown, Portland, Oregon. It was the second best thing I ever did, next to devoting my life to Jesus!

My stepdad and uncle both performed our elegant but modest ceremony. We reserved our budget for a spectacular honeymoon in Maui!

For the next eight years, we lived around the country, serving in youth ministry in South Carolina, Nevada and Colorado. When necessary, I delivered pizzas, assembled industrial air conditioners on night shift and managed Blockbusters. Kim also worked off and on as a dental assistant.

Along the way we had our daughters, Hannah in 2002 and Elliana in 2006. (And we're hopeful to bring home our adopted sons, Israel and Benji, from Haiti this year.)

In 2006, Pastor Sam entrusted me to pastor the youth of Freedom Life Christian Center full time. Since then, Kim and I have watched a generation of kids grow from their insecure middle school years to confident young adults burning with a love for God and serving in the church. I've been honored to bless some as they head to college and train others to be adult youth leaders. I've even performed their marriage ceremonies.

Today, as Freedom Life's Next Gen pastor, I have the privilege to serve God and families by overseeing ministry to kids age birth through young adult. Kim is also the Preschool Director and we are excited to see what God will unfold in the lives of the next generation of students.

Above all, we pray they hear God's fatherly voice speak to their hearts.

Stop. You know I love you.

The Good Child

Valerie Englerth's Back Story

The City of Lancaster reverberated with life. Signals loosed traffic down our block, occasional tires thump-thumping over the sewer grate. Day and night, ambulances sirened to Lancaster General Hospital, up the street from our neighborhood teaming with kids. After school, we made a beeline for the YMCA across the street to play basketball, knock hockey and foosball. We walked to the corner mom-and-pop store for big honkin' wads of bubble gum, candy cigarettes and chocolate. In the summer, bats swooped down in the alley next to our corner row home while we tried to boomerang them with plastic coiled key chains. It was my concrete Garden of Eden.

I was born in March 1981, into the best of homes. My father worked swing shift on the production line making Armstrong flooring, and my mother waitressed at Lombardo's restaurant in the city. My brother, Josh, was three years older than me.

Summers brought vacations at Uncle Babe's cabin in Slate Run with my aunts, uncles, cousins and grandparents on my father's side. Birthdays and holidays brought us together throughout the year, too.

For generations, Dad's family took up some serious pew space at Ross Street United Methodist Church, though Dad and Mom were conspicuously absent from the pack. Still, every Sunday, Mom dolled me up in a girly dress and my brother in slacks and a dress shirt, and sent us on our way with Grandma and Grandpa.

"I hate wearing dresses!" I declared, always an outspoken child. I couldn't wait to see my grandparents and didn't mind church — I just hated fussy clothes.

"Whenever you get tired of going, you just let us know, and you don't have to go," my parents assured us. They didn't like church, so they didn't expect us to like it either.

At church, Jesus was a cutout on the felt board illustrating stories in Sunday school. At home, God was dead, but his storybook values were alive. *Be honest. Help others. Be generous.* And most of all, *be a good person.* If Felt Jesus was real, I figured he wanted me to be a good girl, just like my parents did.

Mom continued to work second shift at Lombardo's and Dad worked swing shift. We had babysitters every third week, when Dad was second shift, too. The rest of the time, Dad was home after school and evenings.

After school, I'd burst through the door, plop my book bag on the floor and unbuckle my super-cool, fluorescent orange, crossing guard strap and badge. "Hi mom," I'd say. A quick snack and a kiss, then I was running out the door for the Y and she was headed to work. Other than that, I only saw Mom on Saturday mornings and Sundays.

I lived for my basketball league at the Y, though I got kicked out of most of the games for fouls. I grabbed, slammed and elbowed opponents without a thought. An aggressive, physical kid, I just couldn't get the hang of not pummeling my adversaries.

Dad, Josh and I played Wiffle ball and kickball in our postage stamp backyard or the alley. If it were raining, we'd use a miniature wooden bat to whack a fabric cat ball around the living room and off the ten-foot ceilings. Sometimes we'd go bowling with Dad's friends. The big treat with Dad was our annual trip to a ball game in Philly or Baltimore with Josh and my cousins, Jeremy and Eric.

The Good Child

Grandma and Grandpa still lived in the Willow Street home where my dad grew up. When the three-bedroom rancher next door went on the market, my parents jumped on it. It was only six miles south of the city, but worlds apart — offering a fresh start for Josh, who had befriended the "wrong" crowd in middle school.

I was 10, and just finished fourth grade when I was snatched off our bustling block to a sleepy suburban neighborhood of retirees. No YMCA. No alley games with neighbor kids, or running in and out of each other's houses to play. My new playground was a finished basement where I immersed myself in V.C. Andrews' *Flowers in the Attic* series and my mother's Danielle Steel novels. I lay awake at night in my hot room with only an occasional cricket chirp or hum of cicadas through the open window to break the silence. *Where have my parents brought me and dropped me off to die?* I wondered.

They took me away from my boyfriend, too — which was probably a good thing considering that at my tenth birthday party, I made out with him in my bedroom closet while my friends ran around the house, playing hide and seek.

"But we *can't* move!" I insisted to my parents. "I love him and I'm gonna marry him someday!" Of course, months later, I'd forgotten all about him.

By the time I started fifth grade at Martin Meylin Middle School, I was chomping at the bit to hang out with kids again. At the same time, I didn't know where I fit in my strange new world. In Lancaster, I walked six blocks to school. Here, I had long bus rides through "Farmville." I was part of the white minority in my city school, but counted on two hands the number of black and Hispanic kids in my new school.

I had also developed ahead of my peers that summer. When I started fifth grade, I was well past training bras — something boys were quick to notice.

"Oops!" a boy said, "accidentally" tripping in the hall and grabbing my chest when he fell. His friends laughed.

"Ha, ha. Very funny," I smirked and walked away. Inside, I wanted to crawl under a rock.

I hid inside oversized shirts and baggy pants, which usually kept boys at bay but alienated the girls who were too catty for me anyway in their established cliques.

"Why did we have to move to this country-fried place?" I ranted at Mom.

"You are beautiful," she stroked my thick, curly brown hair. "And you have a great personality and good heart. People will recognize it, and if they don't, they're not worth your time anyway."

Mom was an incredible encourager, but still, I felt like an outsider.

Josh, on the other hand, found his niche instantly. He excelled at basketball and made fast friends with the popular jock crowd. Mom traded a few evening shifts a week for day shifts bartending so she could see most of Josh's games. Dad never missed one.

"C'mon," Dad beckoned one day when I was about 12. "Let's shoot some hoops." I turned off the TV and my brother and I got up from the couch. "Oh, not you, Val," Dad said. "You're going to lunch and shopping with Mom."

Say what? I hated shopping as much as I hated dresses, and only wanted to "do lunch" if it was a hot dog in the cheap seats. I tried to argue, but mom grabbed her keys and whisked me off to the mall. Everything about it was awkward — the drive, the wandering in and out of stores, the conversation. I just wanted to be with my dad, playing ball.

I was still Daddy's Girl, but things were never the same after that. I wasn't invited to annual ball games anymore. "It's a guy thing," he'd say. "You're going to have a girl's day with your mother." I was suddenly excluded, on the outside, looking in.

Why are you taking me away from Dad? I inwardly raged against my mom. *You haven't been around, and suddenly you want to have mother-daughter time?*

The Good Child

It wasn't until I joined the field hockey team in seventh grade that I started hanging out with classmates. It was nice to be included in team sleepovers and pool parties. We'd go to the budget movie theatre in Willow Street where we could see a second run film for a buck and get an endless tub of popcorn for $3. They were seasonal friendships, though. In the off-season, I was the outsider again, hovering on the outskirts of the social circle with just one or two close friends.

I was a natural at field hockey — aggressive, fast and low. I rocked defense and occasionally played mid-field, too. Dad made it to every game, home and away, and he gave me pointers after each one. He didn't have a clue about field hockey, but he was all in with me. Grandma and Grandpa were regulars in the stands, too, and Mom came to home games when she could. I played through high school, becoming one of the team captains senior year.

I still couldn't play basketball to save my life, but loved it so much that I was the boys' team statistician all four years of high school. I traveled with the team as one of the guys. The only bummer was that I had to wear skirts for games.

Rosie was pretty much my one good friend from seventh through twelfth grade. I spent a lot of time hanging out at her house just a five-minute walk away. Sometimes we made the forbidden trek across the highway to Kmart.

We'd just graduated eighth grade when we made one of our secret trips. This time, Rosie carried a plastic Kmart shopping bag as we walked up and down the aisles stuffing random things in it. We didn't actually want any of the items; we were just bored and thought it was fun. We snatched whitening toothpaste, Band Aids, magazines and — just for laughs — condoms.

"Girls, you're going to have to come with me," a rent-a-cop in plain clothes said, flashing his badge. He walked us to an office in the back and dumped our loot on the desk. The condoms dropped out and all I could think was, *Oh my gosh! Our parents are going to see this!* It definitely gave the wrong impression because we weren't sexually active. In fact, Rosie had never even kissed a boy!

They charged Rosie with shoplifting because she was the one holding the bag. Technically, I was just with her, so they couldn't charge me. They sent me across the street to the barbeque place where Rosie's mom worked.

"Uhm, the security people want you to come over to Kmart," I said.

"What? Is Rosie okay? What happened?" she said, removing her apron hastily.

I struggled to force words from my tightening throat. "Uhm, we kinda got caught shoplifting," I gulped.

She marched me back to Kmart where charges were filed against Rosie and we were released to leave with her mom.

"And we'll be stopping at your house next," Rosie's mom said, eyeing me through the rearview mirror.

Dad had been sleeping just a few hours since coming home off night shift. "You need to go get him anyway," Rosie's mom said. "I'm going to talk to him."

"Uhm, Dad? Rosie's mom is here and she wants to talk to you," I trembled. I just knew this was going to be bad.

He shuffled to the living room, rubbing his eyes. Before she got far into her report, he said, "You need to go to your room."

I scampered off obediently, terrified. Their muffled voices were followed by the sound of the car door slamming and the car pulling out of the driveway and I waited for Dad's footsteps to approach my door. And waited. And waited. I heard the lawnmower. At least an hour passed before my door swung open and I jolted to sit up at attention on my bed.

"I am so disappointed in you, I can't even talk to you," Dad said calmly. He couldn't look at me either. "You just need to stay away from me. I'll talk to your mother about this later."

It was the worst — and ultimately best — thing he could have said to me. To know I'd disappointed him devastated me. I cried my eyes out and stayed in my room until Mom got home and they sat me down at the kitchen table.

"You have completely lost our trust," Dad said. "You are at Ground Zero. We do not trust you to go outside and get the mail at this point. You will do nothing. You will go nowhere, you do not get to go out with friends, you do not get to talk on the phone. You will not turn on the TV without asking. You're going to have to prove to us that you're trustworthy."

Needless to say, it was not a fun summer.

I never got in trouble like that again. I determined not only to be honest, but also to be The Good Child. I went to church with Grandma and Grandpa. I got good grades and became an overachiever at everything. I was always where I was supposed to be and didn't go to a single party. Even peer pressure couldn't sway me.

"What are they for?" I asked my friend, Ashley, when she pulled shopping bags out of the car at the Christiana Mall. They were the paper kind with handles and fancy store logos.

"Oh, these are *good* bags," she said. "In case we find something we want."

"Oh, no. I'm not even going to walk with you guys," I waved my hands in a stopping motion. "Dude, there's no stinkin' way I'm stealing anything again, *ever*. I'll meet up with you later." One of the other three girls wasn't into it either so we hung out together.

As we walked the mall I wondered about the ringleader. *You go to church. You have a Christian family. You read the Bible. What a hypocrite. Maybe Dad's right.*

Dad rejected church in the name of hypocrisy. He complained that churchgoers put on a show on Sundays, yet lived with low standards the rest of the week. So what difference did church make? How could God be real? Dad could have morals and integrity without him. "Just be a good person," he'd say.

Dad even broke family tradition, refusing to have me baptized as a baby. One had to admire his integrity to stand up for his convictions. "Why should I stand in front of the church and promise to raise you to love God, when I know I'm not even going to take you to church?" he reasoned.

But at 14, I made the choice to get baptized. I really connected with the pastor we had at the time. Pastor Nina was a sweet, single woman in her 40s who gave sermons about real life, not highfalutin ideals. I didn't feel like I had to be a perfect, holy person around her. Her Jesus wasn't made of felt — he was her very real best friend. I wanted what she had, and figured getting sprinkled on the head was the way to get it.

The United Methodist Church moves its pastors every few years, and Pastor Nina was replaced with an old guy who bored me. He wasn't a bad guy, but I unfairly compared him to Pastor Nina so, of course, he didn't measure up. But I still put on khakis and a nice shirt and went to church most Sundays anyway, as part of my mission to be Miss Goody Two-Shoes. My brother had quit church, and I wanted my attendance to scream, "I'm better than you! Look at me, I'm the Good Child!"

Unlike many of my peers, I didn't have serious boyfriends. The occasional heart-doodled notes would pass in class, declaring we were "going out," but none of these infatuations amounted to more than notes and handholding and none lasted more than a few weeks.

Just one relationship lasted a couple of months. I met the guy my sophomore year when I was a dishwasher at Lombardo's and he was a bus boy. He was the first boy to ever buy me flowers. We were on a company bus trip to New York when he bought the bouquet from a street vendor. But he wasn't very attentive and that was the only gentlemanly thing he ever did.

At Christmastime we went on another Lombardo's trip to Baltimore. As we rode the water taxi, I said, "Man, it's really cold."

"Yeah, it is," he agreed and put on his sweatshirt. When a guy doesn't give you his sweatshirt to keep you warm, it's a pretty good sign he's not the one!

He was also really — and I mean *really* — into Star Wars. We just hung out watching the movies while I thought to myself, *this is the worst relationship ever.* I finally called it quits when he ditched me on Valentine's Day to go to a Star Wars convention in Philly.

In our junior year, my friend Jess invited me to youth group at her church, Victory Chapel. It was something to do, so I tagged along and discovered it certainly was not my grandparents' church! The lights were low and a band played upbeat songs instead of age-old hymns. About 50 kids stood raising their hands, singing, while the cute drummer caught my eye. He had the coolest hair — shaved underneath with chin-length brown ringlets cascading from the top. When I met him in the light, up close, my heart skipped a beat at his blue eyes and long lashes.

"Who's that hottie?" I asked my friend.

"Oh, that's just Casey," she dismissed with a hand wave. "He's a sophomore. I've known him forever. Blech. You don't want to go out with him."

At the end of the night, the youth pastor, Sam, walked up to greet me. "Hey, how are you? I forget your name," he said.

"It's my first week here," I said.

"Well, it's my second week here," he said. So he was trying to get to know people, too!

I'd always been outside the circle, a peripheral friend. Except for Rosie, I had to pursue people to hang out with, and they didn't always reciprocate. Jess seemed to have a bunch of friends at youth group, so maybe this was my chance to finally be tight with a larger circle of friends?

Youth group was a blast and I kept coming back because Pastor Sam was funny and did crazy stuff. He showed random videos — like one of a cartoon alien dancing to Stayin' Alive under a disco ball that fell on her head and killed her. He let kids pour syrup on his head for winning a contest and he had the senior boys put on a fashion show to show the girls what was inappropriate to wear. I laughed until my ribs hurt as they paraded across the stage in mini skirts, midriffs, and low-cut shirts!

Within a few weeks of my noticing Casey, Jess started hanging out with him a lot. They didn't call it dating, but it was.

"What? I tell you I like a guy and you have to go out with him?" I joked with her. It didn't last long, but I just looked at him as one of our friends after that because of that unwritten code that you don't go out with your friend's ex-boyfriend.

That summer, a bunch of us from youth group went to the New Holland Fair, to ice-skating and to each other's houses to hang out. My parents weren't thrilled about me going to this strange church, but my new friends were good kids, so they let me go. I wasn't allowed to join them on the Back-to-School Retreat at the end of the summer, though.

Jess returned from the retreat radically different because she had decided to go all in with this Jesus stuff and asked her parents to transfer her to a Christian high school. I missed her at school and felt like she left me. But I was still included in the youth crowd without inviting myself. I wasn't just Jess's friend tagging along. I was an insider now!

During senior year, my friend Jess started dating a guy from youth group, Chris Allgyer. Chris had graduated and was attending a technical school in York.

On the night before my 18th birthday, Jess, Chris and a bunch of our friends hung out at my house to celebrate by watching a movie and grubbing on my mom's yummy homemade lasagna.

The next morning, I decided to break from my Golden Child mission just this once and play hooky for my birthday when, mid-morning, the phone rang.

"Val, I'm at the school," Jess' stepmother said. "I need to tell you something. Is anybody at home with you?"

Oh no! I'm busted! I am going to be in so much trouble! My mind raced.

"No," I replied slowly.

"Well, I'm going to come over there."

"What's wrong? Is Jess okay?" I asked.

She paused. "No, Jess is not okay. Chris had an asthma attack and died in his sleep last night."

While I waited for her to arrive, I called my mother at work. I was so hysterical that she couldn't understand me and rushed home.

One by one our tight peer group filed into the Allgyer's house to offer condolences that day. Later that week, we took up entire pews at the funeral at Ridgeview Mennonite Church where the pastor officiated, but invited Pastor Sam to assist him. Chris' youngest brother, Brandon, who was about 11 at the time, sobbed in my arms while the congregation sang "How Great Thou Art."

Really, God? You let an 18-year-old good person go to sleep and not wake up? If God was real, then I was furious with him!

I went to Victory Chapel the following Sunday and sat in the tiny balcony with my friends as usual. We stood for the singing, and I couldn't get the words out.

Man, I wish Chris were here with us. God, why did you have to do this?! I thought, waves of grief and anger crashing over me until I could hardly stand.

Then I heard it — a voice deep within my heart, but not mine at all.

"He is so much happier with me. He doesn't miss being with you." I knew it was God speaking directly to me. "I have him, he's fine."

"I'm so angry at you! How could you let this happen?" I screamed back inside.

His reply was gentle. "Someday you will understand. But right now, know that I can handle you being mad at me. It's okay. I love you."

I dropped to my knees, bawling.

The Bible stories and sermons about how Jesus gave his life so God could forgive me were suddenly real. I realized that being good wasn't good enough.

"I'm sorry for blaming my parents for ruining my life. I'm sorry for thinking I'm better than everyone else. I've been conceited and arrogant thinking I'm a good person. The only one good is you," I cried, tears dripping on the maroon carpet. "I'm done, God," I wept. "It's not my life anymore, it's yours."

Jesus wasn't on a felt board anymore. He was in my heart.

A switch was flipped. I spent every free minute with my church friends and dropped all other activities. On Saturday nights, we slept over at the Allgyer's home. "I don't know what I would do if I lost all of you, too," his mother said. I was always on the go and never wanted to be at home.

I thought, *I'm a Christian now, so I've gotta save everybody* so I came off as Holier Than Thou, and offended my family. I wounded my mother deeply when I told her that I didn't want to see her go to hell. My heart was in the right place, but my words were wrong.

She had already visited my church and it was radically different from the dress-to-the-nines and sing-a-few-hymns services she knew from her Catholic upbringing and Methodist in-laws. Some people waved colored flags during the singing. Then someone babbled out loud in a spooky language. At prayer time, a couple of people fell down on the floor and just lay there.

"What is this place you are going to, Val?" she asked. "Are you sure it's not some kind of cult?"

Becoming a Jesus Freak widened the divide between my family and me. But they tolerated it. "Yeah, we'll see how long this lasts," Dad said.

Until my God encounter in the balcony, I was determined to be the first person in my family to graduate college. I was going to show everyone and be a lawyer and change the world. I was going to reach for the stars and be more "good" than everyone else.

Now, in March of my senior year, I wanted to nix college and spend a year or two doing missionary work with Youth With a Mission, or go to a two-year Bible institute such as Christ for the Nations. I wanted to serve others, and be a homemaker who was ever-present for my husband and kids.

I confiscated a University of Pittsburgh acceptance letter from the mailbox. A few days later, I sat on Grandma's footstool and burst out my confession while she rocked in her puffy brown swivel rocker.

"I ... got ... accepted," I said, gasping for breath between words. "And I can't tell Dad and Mom and I don't know what to *doooo!* It's not fair!"

In her usual peaceful wisdom, Grandma helped me muster the courage to tell my parents.

I might as well have killed someone in cold blood.

"I understand you want to do these things, but you just need to think about it," Mom said. They tried to be calm, but my Jesus Phase had just crossed the line.

"Well, Valerie," Dad said in his usual levelheaded tone. "Right now you've changed your mind about a lot of things that you had already committed to. You owe it to yourself to at least try college for one year."

"But I want to go to YWAM," I pushed.

"We're not paying for that, or for anywhere else that you won't get a degree," he dug in his heels.

I went to Pastor Sam's office. Surely he'd be on my side!

"It's just not fair!" I insisted.

"Well, Val, it *is* biblical for you to go to college," he counseled. "You need to obey your parents. You will show them something by your obedience and your attitude. And God can do great things in you while you're away. It will show you if you really believe what you say you believe."

I went to see Mrs. Allgyer, too. She said the same thing, adding, "You have to understand that with your decision to be a follower of Jesus, your parents have lost a part of you. They don't understand. You need to be kind and obedient to them."

Ugh! It just wasn't fair! But I did what all the adults in my life unanimously advised and enrolled in Poopy Pitt.

I made the most of that summer with my Christian friends. We played mini golf, went rollerblading, played street hockey, ice-skated and went out to eat. We went swimming at the Allgyer's house.

We also went to a weekend youth rally called Acquire the Fire at a stadium in Baltimore. Pastor Sam had gotten us a "great deal" on motel rooms. The floors, counters and furniture were sticky, the bathrooms were grimy and the rooms reeked of stale cigarettes and were so gross that we put towels over the beds and slept in our clothes! But we all thought it was hilarious and had fun with it.

The event was also my baptism into Christian music, and man was it bad! I was into Bruce Springsteen, Rod Stewart and the Stones. Classic rock all the way!

The band Delirious took the stage and my friends were screaming, "Oh, my God, it's Delirious!"

"Wa, wa, wa, who cares?" I teased. We laughed.

That summer, Casey and I became very close friends. He always seemed to go out with crazy girls who loved drama. "Man, I wish I could find a girl that's just like you," he'd say sometimes. I hadn't thought of him romantically since the night I saw him drumming but now, I was giving him a second look.

At college, I joined a Southern Baptist campus organization called The Cross Seekers where I made a lot of friends. I joined them Sundays at a Southern Baptist Church that had a preacher with tidy, uber-short hair and was never seen out of a suit and tie.

Barely five-foot-one, he stood on a box to see over the pulpit and preached in a thick southern draw. I thought I would need an interpreter!

The church had an adopt-a-student program and a sweet family with two adorable little boys picked me. They'd have me over for home-cooked meals and bring me snacks for the dorm.

My new friends and I often used our meal plan flex cards to by bread and lunchmeat, make sandwiches, and take them to homeless people on the streets of Pittsburgh. I was doing good things, but for the first time, I wasn't saying "Look at me! I'm The Good One!" I genuinely felt God's love for these people and wanted them to feel it, too. I wanted them to thank *God*, not me. I wanted them to know *God* was good.

Pastor Sam was right — the year would show that my decision to follow Jesus was more than a phase like my parents hoped it was.

At the same time I grew spiritually, I grew homesick and depressed. Casey and I exchanged letters and e-mails and I talked to him on the shared dorm phone sometimes. When I came home for our friends' wedding during fall break, I told him I had strong feelings for him. He felt the same way!

Wow! This is great! We're officially in a relationship now, I thought.

Then came the "just friends" speech right before I left for school.

"Uhm, I've been thinking that, you know, I'm still a senior in high school and I don't know if a long-distance relationship is a good thing," he said. "We should just be friends."

"Fine! Great! That sounds *awesome!*" I said sarcastically.

Back at school, I ignored Casey's e-mails, letters and phone calls. He wasn't getting the time of day from me!

Three weeks later, I came home for Christmas break when Casey invited some of our friends to his house and asked me to join them and come early. I gave in and met him, standing in his driveway.

"I'm an idiot," he groveled. "I'm sorry. I missed you. I do want a relationship."

Yes! I thought to myself with an imaginary fist pump. On the outside, I played it cool, standing as tall as I could in my 5' 2" frame.

"Well, are you sure this time? Because you said you did, then you said you didn't," I was a bit snide.

"Yes, I'm dumb," he confessed.

"Yes, you are, but that's okay, 'cause I like you," I smiled and threw my arms around his neck.

We continued our long-distance courtship and I couldn't wait to see him on spring break. He took me to Texas Roadhouse where he planned to give me a gift.

"How are you?" said our waitress, Becky, plopping down at our table. She was one of our crowd, and also had dated Casey briefly a few years before.

She was excited to see us and wanted to catch up with me. Each time she came back to wait on us, she'd strike up friendly banter. Meanwhile, I noticed a wretched look on Casey's face.

When she left for the third or fourth time, I asked, "What is your problem?"

"Nothing! Can't she just go do something and leave us alone?"

"I haven't seen her in a while and she's just being friendly. I don't see what's wrong with that," I was taken back by his irritation.

Afterward, we went back to his parents' house, surrounded by 300 acres of farmland belonging to his extended Mennonite family. We walked about a quarter mile up the rural road, past the freshly plowed tobacco field to the Amish one-room schoolhouse. It was dusk and we swung on the wooden swings.

"Val, I have something for you," he said.

"Okay," I kept swinging, looking out over the countryside. Farmland didn't disturb me anymore. In fact, I kind of liked it.

"Uhm, I kinda need you to stop swinging and look at me though," he said.

I dragged my feet in the dirt to stop and twisted the swing to face him. He pulled out a ring with small diamonds on either side of an oval aquamarine.

"I love you, and I intend to marry you someday. This is a promise of my affection and my intentions," I could hardly see him slip it onto my finger for the tears that flushed my eyes.

From the moment we started dating, I knew this was the man I would marry. It was a deep knowing, just like I knew Jesus was real that day in the balcony. Casey was my best friend. We would lie in the hammock that hung between a walnut tree and the shed in his backyard and talk for hours. He was the first person I called when something happened — good or bad. This wasn't gushy puppy love. He was The One.

When I got home, I went to the basement where my mom was watching TV. "Look what Casey gave me!" I said, flashing my jewels.

"*What* is that!" she demanded. "An engagement ring?"

"It's just a promise ring."

"Are you telling me this is an engagement ring? What's a promise ring?"

"I don't know," I said, the wind out of my sail. "It just means we like each other and maybe want to get married someday."

"Alright," she backed off. "As long as you're not talking about getting married."

"No."

Not yet, I thought to myself.

My parents hoped this Jesus thing was a phase and once I immersed myself in college life, I'd get my senses back. Instead, I finished the year with my convictions intact. I was not returning to school and took a job as a groundskeeper for the school district.

It was spring of 2000, and I was home for good, but Casey had just graduated and left for mechanic school near Chicago in July. He hated being away from home even more than I did.

One night at the end of August, my eyelids were heavy as I lay in bed with the phone to my ear. "Well, I'll talk to you tomorrow. I'm going to sleep now," I told him.

"Wait!" he said.

The next thing I heard was panting, like he was out of breath.

"What are you doing?" I asked.

"Just hang on," he gasped. Was he running somewhere?

This went on for several minutes. "Just hold on, I want to do this right."

Finally, he caught his breath.

"I'm at my favorite spot in front of this fountain in a little park," he said. "I come to sit here next to the trees and shrubs and think about you, and about home."

"Oh," I yawned.

"I'm down on one knee and I'm asking you: Will you marry me? I want to spend the rest of my life with you."

Suddenly, I was wide-awake. "Yes!"

I drove to Chicago with his parents to visit him Labor Day weekend. He took me to the park and repeated his proposal in person.

Casey's parents were thrilled, but I met less enthusiasm at home.

I walked into our tiny kitchen and sat on the antique stool against the wall. Dad was washing dishes and Mom was putting dinner leftovers in the fridge.

"So, Casey proposed and we're getting married," I said.

Mom and Dad stopped what they were doing and looked at me and there was a long pause.

"Well," Dad quipped. "You would think a good Christian boy would have asked me for your hand first."

"Oh my gosh, when were you thinking?" Mom asked.

"We're thinking over Memorial Day weekend, when he has a break from school," I said.

"Oh my gosh, that's in like eight months!" Mom said. She was having a bird thinking about all the plans that had to be made.

It took a while for my parents to warm up to the idea that, at 19, I had dropped out of college and my only ambition was marriage and family. Mom married and had Josh and me when she was young so she wanted something different for me.

Casey and I talked about eloping. After all, it was just a day and I didn't need all the hoopla that went with it. But my parents had eloped and wanted me to have a traditional wedding. Their feelings mattered to me and I still didn't want to disappoint them.

When it came to planning the wedding, Mom was amazing. We did some things together, but mostly she took care of every detail to make it beautiful.

"What about these flowers?" she asked, pointing to a florist's catalogue page.

"I like wildflowers. Whatever you pick is fine with me, I don't really care," I said.

"Do you like this cake, or that one?" she asked at the bakery.

"You pick. As long as it tastes good and has the topper I picked out on it, I'm happy," I said.

Casey left school in October, physically homesick and underweight. He transferred to a mechanical school in Exton, where he could commute and worked various mechanic jobs to put himself through school.

Mom always told me, "You can only have that first time once. Make sure the person you give that gift to is worth it and doesn't take it like it's no big deal, because it is."

Mom had been there. Dad and Mom lived together with no plans for marriage when she got pregnant with my brother, Josh.

When she was a few months along, they were at Grandma and Grandpa's house chatting when Grandpa said his peace.

"Enough is enough," he interrupted, addressing my dad. "You are going to respect this young lady. You say you love her? Then you will not let her have this child and not marry her. She is worth so much more than that and if you don't see it, you don't deserve her."

It was the first time a man ever stood up for Mom, and she was touched by the concern of her soon-to-be father in-law. They were very close after that.

Mom's counsel resounded in my ears over the years, and I took it to heart until ...

Casey and I planned to go camping with a group of friends but one by one they bailed out for various reasons. The wise thing would have been to ditch the trip but we went anyway — alone — and caved into temptation and had sex.

We both felt guilty, and vowed not to let it happen again. But we set ourselves up to fail a few more times during our engagement.

In February 2001, I learned I was pregnant.

Oh crap! People are going to know we messed up. They're going to know I'm not The Good Girl.

I burst into tears when I told Casey. "It's fine," he assured. "Everything will be fine. We can do this."

A few days later, we sat down with his parents, Tim and Sally, in their living room and Casey broke the news. I was horrified that we would be a black spot on their uber-Christian Mennonite extended family.

"I'm just so sorry," I hung my head. "I know this will reflect poorly on you."

Sally's soft answer surprised me.

"You're not the first people to have done this. The only thing that's different is that people will know. You aren't the first ones to stumble in life and if people look down on you, they have no standing to judge. None of us is perfectly good all of the time." Tim reinforced her sentiments and they quickly moved on.

"I'm going to be a grandmother!" Sally burst with joy.

When God spoke to me in the balcony, I realized he could forgive me and help me move on. Now, this overwhelming display of love showed me that people could forgive and accept me, too.

Things didn't go down so well when we told my parents, though. Once again, I joined them in the kitchen during dinner cleanup, this time with Casey at my side.

"I have something to tell you," I began. They turned to look at me and, by their expressions, I think they anticipated my next words. "I'm pregnant."

Dad leaned back on the counter and shook his head. "Well, so much for you dating a Christian boy," he scoffed.

Mom burst into tears. "I don't understand. I'm too young to be a grandmother."

Why do you even care? I thought. *You have no belief system to renounce having a baby before marriage. How could you take it badly?*

I guess, for them, it was history repeating itself. Casey and I were 19, soon to be 20. Casey was still in school and I had no career and no degree. They knew from experience that it wouldn't be easy and wanted more for me.

We married in May 2001 and moved into a basement apartment in Casey's grandparents' home. Our daughter, Hallie, was born in October that year. We scraped by to pay school loans, pay hospital bills and buy groceries but God saw us through it, like he had done all my life.

We lived there for almost three years and had our second daughter, Mia, in 2004. We rented an apartment in Willow Street then, to be closer to my parents. After about a year and a half, we started looking for a house, but everything in our price range was a dump.

Meanwhile, Tim and Sally were empty nesters talking about downsizing. They didn't really want to leave their home, but it seemed like the financially sound thing to do. After much discussion, they agreed to let us move in and start buying the house from them. It was a win-win for all of us.

Changing the world through a legal career is a noble aspiration. But for me, that dream wasn't about serving others; it was about impressing others to validate myself. It was about saying, "Look at how good I am!"

Today, I want to serve others, starting with my husband and daughters. I was there for my daughters' first steps and first words. I have a loving, hard-working husband who I want to spend time with.

I helped with everything I could at church, including teaching kids in the 3- to 5-year-old class (felt board not included). After a few years, Pastor Sam became the lead pastor of our church, which had been renamed, Freedom Life Christian Center. The new youth pastor, Jake, asked me to be a youth leader.

"I don't like teenagers. They're scary," I said.

But he's a very convincing fella, so I pitched in by hiding out in the youth café talking to other adults. After a while, Jake announced a mission trip to London. I couldn't go to YWAM for a year, but I could certainly go to London for ten days! This meant that I had to work with the small group of students preparing for the trip and, as I got to know them, they didn't seem so scary anymore.

I always wanted a nickname, and at the end of the trip, I finally got one when the group leader in London led us in reflection of our experience before flying home.

"Let's go around the room and each person pick another team member. Tell them what animal they would be, and why," she said.

One of the students called me out. "Val, you are a Mama Cheetah. That's because you are loving and cuddly and fun, but if anyone messes with your cubs, you will be fierce."

Yes, I loved these kids. And if anyone messed with them, I'd be fierce!

After that, I opened our home to the kids to come hang out. We had discussions about hot topics and challenged them to know why they believed what they said they believed. Casey taught Brian to ride a 1944 Allis Chalmers tractor in our yard and I helped teach Cindy how to drive. Kids watched UFC fights on beat-up sofas in our basement and I baked them cookies and other yummy things. I wanted them to feel welcome, like they belonged.

I've had the privilege of watching these kids grow into amazing young adults who show their faith in how they live. Today, I get to show God's love and fierce protection to the next generation as Elementary Director at church.

My parents wanted "more" for me, and I have it. I have rich, authentic relationships. I get to bring God's love and hope to families by working with children and their parents. I once wanted to change the world, but I found something that trumps that dream. I'm part of what *God* is doing to change the world, one precious life at a time. And that's the greatest honor I could ever receive.

Wounded Knees
Callie's Back Story

Chase and his friend, Doug, sat on the sofa in our rented West End cottage. A pistol lay on the coffee table where they were rolling joints and cutting lines of crystal meth.

"You're a piece of sh**!" I shouted at Chase, unconcerned about waking our two sleeping children. My heart grew as dark as the night outside as yet another argument escalated. *This isn't the life I planned with my high school sweetheart,* I thought.

"What the f*** is your problem?" Chase demanded.

"You're no good! I can't believe you're doing this! You're on probation, you could get serious time!" My volume surged with my fury. "Just get out!"

Chase bolted from the sofa, slammed me against the wall, and landed a rock hard slap to the side of my skull. As I lifted my woozy head, his penetrating eyes arrested my scattered thoughts and I knew . . .

The monster was back.

I was born in August 1977, and lived in Gap, Pennsylvania, with my parents and sister, Dana. Dana was four years older than me and was born during my mother's first marriage.

After several moves, we settled into a twin home in Atglen. My mother's parents moved from Arizona to a house apartment a short walk away while I started first grade at Octorara Elementary School.

Mom worked at the Servicstar warehouse in Parkesburg, and tended bar at Friendly Tavern in Christiana. Dad was also a bartender there, and never had what Pop Pop considered a "real" job. Yet, Dad always had cash — and lots of it. I didn't ask where it came from and he didn't tell. But some school mornings, I would walk in on an all-night poker game lingering in our kitchen. And when I was 12, I saw him exchange a cash-stuffed briefcase with a man at the tavern pool table.

Pop Pop greeted us at the bus stop each day, chain-smoking Camel non-filters in his massive Army-green station wagon. We'd stop at the Atglen post office to check his mailbox. Then we went to his house, where he helped us with homework. I watched him craft wooden napkin holders and flower boxes to sell at Atglen Market. I chatted with Grammy in the kitchen.

Sometimes Pop Pop drove us to our house where Grammy was making our beds, putting in laundry, and starting dinner for my mom. Without fail, Pop Pop set the day's Help Wanted section prominently on the kitchen table.

"When you gonna get a d**n job?" he'd often bark at Dad.

"I told you, I'm retired," Dad would say. It was a dispute that Pop Pop would never win.

When I was 12, I walked home from the bus stop alone for several weeks while Pop Pop was in the hospital. The doctors said he had emphysema, but I was assured my hero would be home soon.

One day, I came home to silence, lights on and a warm casserole on top of the stove as if someone left abruptly. Dana had beaten me home and came bounding down the stairs, unconcerned.

"Where is everyone?" I asked.

"I don't know. I just got home. I'm waiting for my friend to pick me up," she said.

Ten minutes later, I stepped out onto the porch as my mother pulled her car to the curb. She helped my red-faced grandmother out of the car and shuffled her toward the house, tissues in hand.

"What's going on?" I gasped as the storm door smacked shut behind me. Grammy struggled to navigate the porch steps as she drew stilted, heaving breaths.

"He's gone," Mom shook her head. "Pop Pop's gone." The words sucked the air out of my lungs and left a hole in my gut. *What do you mean he's gone?* I thought. *Where did he go?*

As the answer to my unspoken question hit hard, I turned on my heels and ran into the house. I raced up the stairs to my room, slamming the door behind me to fend off the truth that pursued. Sobbing, I threw myself on the bed.

The center of my universe was gone and I had no idea where he went. I didn't have religion. In fact, I'd never been in a church. I imagined people could come back from the dead, be reincarnated or become demons or ghosts like I'd seen in movies. *Would those things happen to Pop Pop? Could he still see me?*

I had nightmares and tremors for weeks after the funeral. I dreamt of Pop Pop was picking me up in his monstrous station wagon. As I got in the car, I realized it wasn't my idol in the driver's seat, but a ghastly, mangled doppelganger. I even thought I saw him at the post office and heard him on the phone! *Was he trying to contact me from the dead?* I wondered.

It was a long time before Grammy went back to her apartment and she stayed with us for a while. Before Pop Pop died, they had reserved a unit in Glen Brook Apartments, a small complex under construction in the neighborhood. She moved there about four months after the funeral.

Mom and Dad sent Dana and me to bed each night at 9:00 and left for the tavern. Dana's friends would show up to smoke and listen to music until my parents served last call. By the time I was 12, I hung out with Dana's peers more than she did. They drove, so we'd go to Springdale Deli, or my house or anywhere else that parents weren't around. We often stopped at the bar to see my dad who would unfold a wad of cash from his pocket and snap off some bills for me. I'd pitch in for gas and we'd cruise around Atglen and Christiana looking for something to do.

Gradually, Dad stopped coming home at night. Sometimes I couldn't sleep and would get up for a drink. As I reached the bottom of the stairs, I'd see the fiery head of mom's cigarette as she dragged on it in the dark. No television. No lights. Just a cancer stick and a broken heart, waiting for her husband to come home from who-knows-where.

They divorced when I was 13, after my mother discovered Dad was having an affair with her friend. Dad stayed in the house, Mom moved in with a friend, and I went to live with my grandmother. Dana had already moved in with her boyfriend after getting pregnant and dropping out of school her senior year. In my 13-year-old mind, it didn't get better than this. I could live next door to my best friend, Jane, with my beloved Grammy who thought I could do no wrong.

One day, as I waited at Dad's house for my sister, her boyfriend, John, flicked a lighter and fired up a joint. "Ever try this?" John passed it my way after taking a long drag.

"No," I admitted, eagerly taking my first hit.

We finished the joint, but I didn't feel any different. *What's the big deal?* I wondered.

"Here's another one. You can smoke it with your friends," he said. I couldn't wait to share it with Jane, although I still wasn't sure what the big deal was.

The next day I pulled my treasure from my pocket as Jane and I walked on the railroad tracks behind my dad's house. "Look what I got," I said.

We lit up and this time I got completely stoned! We couldn't stop laughing. We went to Jane's to eat mounds of ice cream and all the munchies we could find. Jane peed her pants laughing. Then I peed my pants laughing at her. Our ribs hurt the next day from laughing so hard. That summer between seventh and eighth grade,

I babysat often for Dana and John's daughter — always in exchange for a few bucks and a joint.

Jane and I met new people as we walked the streets of Atglen that summer with nothing to do but smoke. We especially liked hanging out with a group of older black guys. One of them was Darren, an 18-year old drug dealer who took us to parties where we smoked joints, drank 40s and snorted coke. I was 13, drunk and willing, the first time we had sex.

Getting drugs and seeing Darren were never a problem because Dad still handed me money, and I'd steal from him, too. By the time school started, I was telling my parents and Grammy that I was babysitting for my nephews in Lancaster on the weekends, and staying at Darren's instead.

One day, the television news caught my eye. "Two men have been arrested and charged today with robbing the Bank of Lancaster County in Gap ..." It was Darren and his brother.

Soon after, Dad caught wind I'd been seeing Darren and was writing him in prison. As I tiptoed down the stairs, I overheard him on the phone, hiring someone to break Darren's legs. "You don't have to break them both, just one," he said. Never mind that Darren was 18 and I was 13, or that he was a drug dealer and a criminal. My dad went off the hook because I was with a black guy. I wrote Darren to warn him and end our fling.

I met Cameron in my sophomore year at Octorara Area High School. He was a senior with decent looks, a Camaro and lots of pot. What more could 15-year-old party girl want? We got high together and started hooking up.

I missed a period.

"Guess what?" I asked Cameron as we smoked a bowl in his car on the way to a graduation party. "I took a test and I'm pregnant."

"What? That's f***ed up," he said in stoner slow motion. "What are we gonna do? That ain't cool."

"I'm not having a baby, just so you know," I said, taking another hit off the pipe.

"Well, how much will something like that cost?" he asked.

The abortion cost $380 and required parental consent so I had to tell my mother. She and Cameron took me to a large clinic in Harrisburg where we joined 50 others in a dreary waiting room with cold white floors and a foul smell. I took a seat on one of the metal folding chairs and wondered about the other women. Some paced. Others fought with boyfriends. Some cried. At 15, it seemed I was the youngest in the room; most looked to be at least in their 20s. *Why don't they have their babies?* I wondered.

My turn in the assembly line came and they knocked me out with anesthesia. When I came to, the nurse sent me on my way with a ginger ale, crackers and pain pills for cramps. "I'm starving," I told my mom. "Let's stop at Subway."

The event was never discussed again. *That wasn't bad*, I thought. *If I get pregnant again, somebody better just dollar up and I'll do it again.*

I dumped Cameron a few months later, when he got busted for being high at school and ratted out the three of us who smoked the weed with him. One of these guys was Chase, a junior who just transferred in from Coatesville Area Senior High School.

Everyone loved Chase's car, Chase's weed and Chase's blond curls — especially me. He took me for rides in his white '88 Jeep Raider. By the end of that summer before my junior year, we were the Octorara equivalent of Brangelina. Everyone wanted to be us.

A few months into the school year, a guy named Rob was hitting on me at my locker. "Chase is a looser," he said, leaning on the next locker. "Go out with me, Callie. A while back, you said you would."

"I'm with Chase. I'm not interested," I said, slamming my locker shut.

Rob's tone changed as he moved closer. "He's a d***! And you said you'd go out with me!"

Chase was walking up and overheard. "Dude, don't do this," he warned, stepping between us. Rob leaned around Chase and spit on me.

Chase went at him like a pit bull in a dogfight. They landed hard blows to each other and grappled on the floor. Finally, a teacher hollered, "In the office! Now!"

They marched, seething, into the reception area, Chase first. Rob jumped him again from behind. Like a bar brawl in a movie, they rolled onto the reception desk, crashing its accessories to the ground and Chase pounded my antagonist until the principal pulled them apart and called police. An ambulance took Rob to the hospital.

It was Chase's third strike at Octorara, and he was out. He went back to Coatesville briefly, but he was desperate to graduate with our friends at Octorara that year. After much begging and bargaining, the principal laid out conditions and let him return.

After graduation, no amount of pleading and pouting swayed my mom to let me go to senior week in Ocean City, Maryland. Chase and I had been inseparable. Now, I clung to him as he packed his car to leave. I tried to turn on a pouty charm in my white Daisy Duke shorts, pink tank top and Keds.

"I really don't want you to go," I whined, drawing my finger down his arm.

"Just come," he said.

"Really?"

"Yeah. What's the worst that could happen?" he shrugged.

I hopped in the car.

Six of us shared a hotel suite the first night. The next day, our crowd grew to 30 kids smoking weed, drinking beer, dropping acid and eating mushrooms. That afternoon, a stern pounding on the door startled us.

"OCMD Police! Open the door!"

46

"Sh**!" someone yelled. "Put your stuff away!" Everyone scrambled to hide or flush their substances.

The cops rolled in to find open alcohol everywhere in our suite full of under-21s. Those 18 and older were arrested, cuffed with zip ties and crammed into a paddy wagon.

An officer stood tall in front of me, one hand on his shiny black belt. "Are you Callie?"

"No," I said timidly, wondering how he knew my name.

"Then what's your name?" he demanded authoritatively.

I couldn't think on my feet, so I fessed up. "Callie."

"Come with me," he said as he took me by the arm and put me in the back of his cruiser with Jim, the only other minor from our room.

"What is going on?" I asked Jim.

"I don't know," he said. "But Tim had like 13 sheets of acid on him."

The officer slid behind the wheel and looked in the rearview mirror. "I hope you know, Callie, that you are officially a missing person," he said soberly. "We found you here because your boyfriend's mother told your parents where you were staying. So yes, *you* are responsible for this hoe-down."

"Oh my God! People are being arrested because of me!" I was shocked.

"Aww, I wouldn't go back to school if I were you," Jim shook his head.

I was devastated. I didn't care what my family would do, but I was terrified of what my friends would think. It was the first time I ever though about a consequence to my actions; it was also the last one for a while.

Dad retrieved me without a word and for the next three hours, we drove in silence and smoked cigarettes. His first words emerged when we were almost home. "You're coming back to my house tonight."

He tossed his keys on the table when we walked in the door, then gave it to me straight. "Your mom wanted me to leave you there. What were you thinking? I know you have a problem. Your mother and I have decided to send you to a 28-day rehab in Chester."

"But I don't have a drug problem," I pleaded to no avail.

We didn't have cell phones then, so I couldn't reach Chase. I couldn't even tell Jane my parents were sending me away because she left to join the continuing party at the shore.

In rehab, I said what staff wanted to hear and did what I was told, but my mind fixed on one thing for the next 28 days: I had to see Chase. I used my scant phone privileges to call his house but his mother hung up on me every time. I later learned that my family did the same to Chase.

Meanwhile, I missed a period.

Dad picked me up from rehab when my time was served.

"I missed my period," I said as soon as we got to his house.

He got back in the car, drove to the store and returned, tossing a pregnancy test on the table. "You're taking this test and you're taking it right now. You cannot have a baby."

When it turned up positive, my first thought was to tell Chase. *Oh, we really are gonna be together forever!* My emotions soared. *It's not puppy love like everyone says. We're meant to be!*

The next day, as my friend Rachel was driving Jane and me to her house in Parkesburg, Chase's Jeep whizzed by us in the opposite direction. Tires screeched as he did a one-eighty and gunned it to follow us. Rachel raced down the road with Chase on our tail. She wasn't about to let me see him before I heard the list of his sins.

Jane gushed the details of Chase's multiple sexual conquests during senior week after he was released on bail. And there were others in the weeks that followed. "He's scum, just forget about him," my girlfriends consoled.

This can't be happening!

It was Pop Pop's death all over again. I tried to process the information but my head was in a fog and my stomach felt like it was just sucked out of my throat.

We parked at the curb in front of Rachel's house and Chase jumped out of his Jeep. "I've been trying to get a hold of you, but ..." he started. I stopped him with a stinging slap to the face.

"I hate you!" I screamed, kicking his car wildly. "I. Can't. Believe you!" I know everything you did! Don't you ever talk to me again!"

"Whoa, whoa, whoa," he said, trying to calm my torrent.

"And by the way," I drew a deep breath. "I'm pregnant!"

I ran into the house and shut the door. Chase pounded on it. "What? Come out here!"

"Chase, you need to go away," Jane said. "Now isn't the time."

My friends joined me in the house, jaws dropped. "You're pregnant? Explain!"

Over the next few weeks, Chase would call me while he was drunk or stoned. "What are you gonna do?" he demanded.

"Don't worry about it," I'd answer. I knew I was keeping the baby, but I wanted to leave him hanging.

The doctor sent me for an ultrasound because I measured larger than I should. Apparently, I was four months along by the time I had missed my period. Now, I was 22 weeks pregnant with a little girl.

"You can live here with the baby and finish school, dear," Grammy encouraged softly. So I nested at home, eating mint chocolate chip ice cream with her every night, still clean and sober since senior week.

Chase, on the other hand, was off the hook with parties and girls. He continued to call me, stoned. "I miss you," he'd say. "Please tell me what's going on."

Eventually, I relented. "Okay, we can get together and talk when you're not high." He came over the next day, sober.

"I really want to be a part of our daughter's life," he said. "And I miss you. Please, let's try and work things out." He had moved in with his friend, Rich, after graduation and was working two good jobs. He certainly had the means to support us. But he was still a drug dealer and a liar.

"I can't trust you," I said. "Let's take it one step at a time."

By the time I was seven months, Chase's charm and concern were winning me over. But something didn't sit right with me when he left my place one day. Jane and a guy we knew stopped by later and I said, "Let's take ride to Chase and Rich's and see what's going on."

As I we walked up to the house where a few people hung out in the yard and on the porch, Chase stumbled out the front door, his neck purple with hickies. I grabbed a beer can from the ground and bashed him over the head with it, knocking him unconscious. I left, and that night someone told me he was sleeping with one of my friends.

The next day the phone rang. "How ya doing?" he asked, as if nothing happened. He didn't remember.

"Are you kidding me?" I screamed. "You're gonna pay!" I let the air out of his tires a few times after that.

A few weeks before our daughter was born, Chase started visiting again. He really did want to be a father, even if I wouldn't hook up with him. He would touch my belly and ask what he could do for me. He didn't party much and played cards with me at night because he didn't want to miss my labor.

At about 11:00 one night, we were playing Rummy at my kitchen table with Grammy and one of Chase's friends when I felt sharp cramps. "I think it's time," I said, bracing myself in the kitchen chair.

Chase had been drinking, so my mom picked us up and took us to the hospital. I labored hard for 25 ½ hours while nurses assured me they were giving me the medication I begged for, but they weren't because Medicaid didn't cover it.

Our daughter was the most beautiful creature I'd ever laid eyes on. I held her close and both families arrived to admire her. I named her Melody, after the tag in a pretty baby dress I had bought. Chase's grandfather picked us up from the hospital in a limo and took us to a big "Welcome Melody" party at Chase's mother's house.

Six weeks later, in April 1995, I returned to school. Chase worked second shift at Servicstar with my mom so he could watch Melody during the day. In May, I learned I wouldn't graduate on time because I failed World Cultures. I could have gone to summer school and graduated, but I didn't.

Instead, I rode in friends' cars, drinking and smoking pot again with Melody nestled in the car seat beside me. When I tucked my daughter into bed at night, I left her with Grammy and went to parties, and when Chase had her for the weekend, I really went wild.

Within a month of Melody's arrival, Chase got two DUIs and started doing crystal meth. He lost his license, had huge fines and spent some weekends in jail. I drove him to court ordered classes and wherever else he needed to go. I just couldn't resist him because he was my best friend and I was still in love. We started getting high together and hooking up again.

"My cousin Bill and I are getting a place in Parkesburg so I can get rides to work. You should move in with me," Chase said, when Melody was almost a year old.

Maybe we are meant to be after all.

I was all in.

The apartment was dark, sunlight repelled by towels hung in the windows. A trail of visitors came at all hours to buy meth and pot, or just hang out and use. They dropped acid and spent hours, even days, wasted in our living room. I started doing meth with Chase.

Chase still managed to hold down his evening job and I started a morning shift waitressing across the street. I popped home on my break one day and was locked out of my apartment while

Melody wailed inside. "Chase!" I pounded and pounded, but he didn't respond. I climbed through a window and found him passed out. This scene played out day after day, so I quit my job.

Then the rapes started.

"I don't want to, baby," I turned my face from Chase as he pinned me to the bed. I was wasted, and tired. Demonic eyes bore through my soul while he ignored my pleas. This couldn't be Chase. This was a terrifying monster with uncanny strength. Melody cried for hours in the crib in the next room while I winced in pain and Chase's meth-induced rush drove him on. By the time I got to our daughter, she'd pulled her messy diaper off and cried herself to exhaustion.

After one of these episodes, I went to Melody's room where I lay on the floor next to her crib. The muffled laughs and voices of our "guests" reverberated through the floor. I thought of how skinny — and terrifying — Chase had become. Melody looked malnourished. *How did I get here?*

"You're a maniac! You're a monster!" I told Chase just seven months after moving in. "I'm leaving!"

"Fine," he said. "Do whatever the h*** you want."

I left with Melody and moved in with my mom and her new husband, Ray. Ray subscribed to something I couldn't wrap my head around: rules. *Why would I have rules? What do they provide for me?*

After six months of conflict with Ray, I turned to my dad again. He bought me a car and put up security for an apartment in Gap. I signed up for subsidized daycare and got a job waitressing at The Brass Eagle near my apartment. I was 19.

Just like my days of wandering Atglen with Jane in junior high, I met a whole new party scene at The Brass Eagle's bar and I started snorting coke again with a coworker. Chase left the Parkesburg apartment soon after I did to move in with his mother. He took Melody every other weekend, so I used my freedom to pick up extra shifts and host after-parties at my apartment.

It was the summer of 1996, and Chase started spending time with me again. I sometimes gave him rides (his license was still suspended). He would get dropped off to see Melody and stay over because I didn't feel like driving him home. Chase had backed off the meth, but we smoked pot together and had sex a couple of times.

I missed a period.

"I'm pregnant," I told him on the phone.

He laughed. "Well, that's a joke. I hope you don't think it's mine."

"Chase, it really is yours." I'd had a one-night stand with someone but the timing wasn't right. This was definitely Chase's baby!

"I ain't buyin' it, Cal. There's no way it's mine," he insisted. "You're not sucking me into that. If you have this baby, I'm gonna get tests!"

Once again, I was farther along than one missed period would suggest. Weeks went by as I barely gave a thought to my plans. I lived in denial of my condition, continued to use drugs, even dabbled with crack.

During that time, I took a nine-to-five job in the loan center of a bank in Downingtown and still worked at The Brass Eagle on the weekends. Coworkers suspected I was pregnant but, since I barely showed, I told them I wasn't.

My denial ended when the baby arrived. "He's definitely mine," Chase beamed as he held our son in the hospital. No one could deny the likeness, right down to Chase's cleft chin.

"Let's name him Trent," he said. "I want to be with you, Callie. I love you and I want to raise our kids together and have a life."

But I was overwhelmed because for nine months, I had convinced myself this wasn't happening and now it was! I needed time to adjust to reality. Chase rented us a small cottage in Coatesville's West End, and my sister took Trent home with her. We took Trent on weekends and when he was 6 months old, he came home to stay.

I was 20 and Chase was 21. On the surface, things were fine. We had good jobs; I worked at the bank and restaurant and he worked at the butter factory. We had two delightful children and a home. We liked each other well enough. We parented our kids. We still got high together, though nothing like the first time we lived together. But we were just going through the motions and our fighting resumed. Two kids and three years later, our pre-senior week magic still eluded us.

Kevin, on the other hand, was interesting and attentive. The IT tech at work, he sat on my desk for small talk after installing updates one day. We shared smoke breaks and increasingly friendly e-mails. I looked forward to work every day, but not for career satisfaction. Lunches graduated to dinner dates while I lied to Chase about working late or hanging out with girlfriends.

Kevin was fun. He wanted to go dancing, hear live music and be around a crowd. All Chase wanted to do was smoke weed, clean his guns and go hunting. Our involvement snowballed fast and Kevin pressed me to leave Chase. But he was coming on too strong and I wasn't ready to take that leap.

I reconsidered one night as Chase and Doug sat on the sofa rolling joints. Chase had taken up meth again and they'd been doing lines. My muscles tensed and my heart pounded as I fought back a bubbling rage until Melody and Trent were fast asleep.

Then, I exploded.

"You're a piece of sh**!" I shouted at Chase.

"What the f*** is your problem?" Chase demanded.

"You're no good! I can't believe you're doing this!" I screamed. "Just get out!"

Chase bolted from the sofa, slammed me against the wall, and landed a rock hard slap to the side of my skull. As I lifted my woozy head, those penetrating eyes arrested my scattered thoughts.

The monster was back.

I dodged him and flew out the back door, slamming it behind me. "9-1-1," I dialed my cell phone with shaking hands.

The cops arrived to find a mark on my face, drugs on the table and Doug cleaning a pistol he had no permit for. Chase was arrested and I was escorted to state police barracks to fill out paperwork. My mother came to stay with the kids.

I sat beside the trooper's desk while he asked me what happened. "This is abuse and Chase is already on probation. We can put him away so he can't do this to you again. Do you want to press charges?" he asked.

Even after all the pain Chase had caused me, I just couldn't it. But when he came home from jail the next day, my bags were packed.

"Why the h*** would you do that to me?" he demanded.

"We both know this ain't working. And I'm seeing someone else," I shot back, hoping it hurt as much as the blow to my head. Chase left the house instead and moved in with his mom.

For the next eight months, Kevin talked about settling down as a family. He wanted his parents to meet my kids. He wanted to get married. He wasn't fun anymore, just clingy.

I missed a period.

My first call was to the abortion clinic in West Chester because there was no way I wanted Kevin to know! The next morning, I dropped the kids off with Chase on the way to have the abortion.

"What time do you want me to drop them off?" Chase asked.

I burst into tears.

"Oh my God? What's going on?" he asked, putting his arm around me.

"I'm pregnant," I sobbed, starring at the floor in shame. "I don't know what's wrong with me."

"Let me take you. My grandmom will watch the kids," he said with all the tenderness I craved.

How could this man ever have been such a monster? On the one hand, he was always there for me. On the other, he used and abused me like an animal.

The stained chairs and a dirty floor at the clinic were almost as unsettling as my condition. The intake assistant said my insurance would cover the abortion, but not anesthesia. I was heading into this one with eyes wide open.

The doctor's instruments tugged painfully inside me. A loud motor hummed as an accordion-like pump sucked pink tissue and blood through a long tube into a glass container. Horror movies flashed through my mind. *Oh my God! I'm going to see an arm, a foot or something!* I didn't, but my heart raced from panic and physical shock. The cramps approached the pain of labor. I felt faint.

Kevin was standing in my driveway when Chase and I pulled up to my house. "What is going on?" he asked.

I'd been looking for an out from our relationship and this was it. "I just had an abortion," I said. "Chase gave me a ride."

"You b**ch!" he shouted, snatching a rock from the flowerbed and throwing it across the yard. "That was my child! What kind of sick woman are you?!"

"Take it easy, man," Chase said. But the rocks and insults kept flying. "He's your boyfriend. You deal with it," Chase said, walking into the house.

Kevin left, but I wasn't rid of him yet. He harassed me at work, even after I reported him. Then a merger at the bank left me without a job and I never heard from him again.

It was 1998 and Chase and I were on again. His uncle bought an ice cream business in Allentown and asked Chase to help him with it for the summer. Chase wouldn't be able to pay my rent while he was gone, so he moved the kids and me to his mother's house and was supposed to come home often.

When Chase stopped coming around as much as he promised, I felt abandoned and asked my dad to find an apartment for me and the kids, now 2 and 4. I landed an accounts receivable job and continued to waitress at The Brass Eagle on weekends and, at 21, was eager to get into clubs legally. I started smoking boogies (marijuana with crushed up crack) and soon picked up the crack pipe.

I also started dating Paul, a respectable business owner with a black Corvette who didn't do drugs and loved my kids. For the first time since high school, I was in love! I wasn't about to mess that up, so I hid my escalating drug use from him.

"What's Paul doing at my daughter's birthday party?," Chase asked as Melody ripped wrapping paper from a present. "Seriously, does he have to be here?" Chase had moved back in with his mother after eight months in Allentown and couldn't stand the thought of me planning a future with someone else. His power over me was broken. He couldn't toy with me anymore.

It was a red light that caused him to take a long, hard look at his life. He sought answers at his grandmother's church, quit drugs and declared that he "surrendered my life to Jesus."

Whatever.

My public life was looking up, but my private world spiraled out of control. I was functional at work and Paul never suspected my addiction. But I smoked crack out my bedroom window while my kids played outside. I smoked it in the kitchen when they went to bed. I didn't go to parties anymore; I used alone. That summer of 1999, I inhaled $500 a day of crack. I stole money from Paul and my dad, even after they gave me plenty to pay my bills. I owed countless people money. My waking thought each morning was, *How am I going to get some crack?*

One day, my boss gave me an extended lunch break to go home for my camera card and renew my driver's license. As I left my apartment, my dealer stopped me in the alley. "Yo, I need a ride to the 'ville," he said. When I dropped him off in Coatesville, he tossed a crack rock on the passenger seat and said, "Thanks for the ride."

Maybe a few hits would be cool before I go back to work?

I smoked it all day, just driving around and stopping in parking lots. I smoked with the windows up, obsessively checking the rearview mirror until the car clock caught my eye at 5:00. I was coming down, and needed more to stave off the crash, but I'd spent my money on gas, and I had to pick up the kids from daycare in an hour.

As I approached the daycare, Chase passed me. He circled back, flashed me down, and then pulled up beside me. "Where you been all day? Your work called your mom and no one can find you."

I hung my head and bawled.

"Look at you, you're a wreck," he said, concerned. "What are you on?"

"Crack," I sniffed, wiping my eyes.

"I will get the kids. Meet me at your mom's," he took charge. "And don't you go off somewhere."

I was hiding, curled up on the shower floor, when Chase arrived. He pulled open the curtain.

"Come on, you can come out here," he coaxed me like a kitten to the living room where Mom waited. Too ashamed to meet their eyes, I stared at the carpet, hugging myself with my boney arms. I weighed 98 pounds.

"You have a problem and we're going to get you into a rehab," Chase said. Once again, nice-Chase was coming to my rescue.

I lay on the sofa while they called around for a rehab with an open bed. Their voices faded away as I crashed into a deep sleep. An hour later, Chase shook me.

"Come on. We're going to get your clothes. You're leaving for Florida in the morning," he said.

My words came slowly. "What? That's too far, and my birthday's coming. I don't want to be in rehab for my birthday."

"It's one birthday, Cal. If you want to be a good mom, you have to do this," he insisted.

"I want to call Paul. I want Paul to take me," I said. Chase didn't care, as long as I got to rehab.

Paul came right over and sat on the couch beside me.

"I don't know what to say," he said quietly. "If I knew, I would've tried to help you." He tucked a cross necklace in my hands, kissed me on the cheek and stood to leave. "Take care of yourself, Callie."

He walked out of the door, and out of my life.

I leaned my seat back and closed my eyes on the flight to Del Ray Beach.

Why is Chase being so nice to me? I wondered. *I love Paul, but he doesn't want me anymore. Am I supposed to be with Chase?* I'd just lost my kids, job and last ounce of self-respect and still my only angst was my love life.

The first week of rehab was orientation to rules, reviewing my drug history and incessant questions from staff about feelings. The second week, I started daily Twelve Step classes and intensive counseling.

I lay on the couch during one of my sessions as my therapist, Sharon, instructed me to close my eyes and picture myself as a little girl on the beach. I had a vivid image of myself in a blue sailor suit with freckles, pigtails and Band Aids on my knees.

"Why is she hurt?" Sharon asked gently. She told me to ask the girl, and I agreed to the role-play.

"She fell down and nothing seems to heal her wounds," I said.

"Okay, Callie. I want you to picture someone who caused those injuries," Sharon guided.

I didn't just *see* the little girl. I *was* her. On the couch, tears streamed from my closed eyes. In my mind, I felt the sand in my toes, smelled the salt air and heard waves hitting the shore. A man with Chase's blue eyes and my dad's nose approached. His face was a hybrid, representing them both.

"Tell them they can't hurt you again. Tell them you won't depend on them to make things better or let them define who you are," Sharon coached.

I was crying, reaching out for the two-faced man to scoop me up and hold me. He turned around, and his face changed — it was Jesus! As he set me on his hip and walked me toward the ocean, tears flowed and my spirit soared.

"Tell me what you see," Sharon pressed me. "How are you going to conquer this?"

I opened my eyes. "Jesus!"

I wasn't looking for religion. I didn't go to church and I didn't know any Bible stories. But this Jesus was as real as the sofa I lay on and I determined to know him.

That Sunday, I hopped on the church shuttle from rehab to a mega church in Ft. Lauderdale with just one other patient, Rob.

"Dude, Ima get my life togetha up in here!" he said, taking a seat and clapping his hands. We laughed.

"Well, don't you leave me alone!" I said.

We entered the massive auditorium through one of its many front doors. A few thousand worshippers were also filing in and we took a seat near the middle. The Florida sun cast soft rays through stained glass windows depicting Jesus in action. In one, he prayed. In another he raised a challis to a dinner party. In another, he held a child on his lap. This was the Jesus I came to find.

During the sermon, I joined Rob in quietly heckling the preacher. I didn't want him to know I was actually listening to him talk of how Jesus could give me joy. But by the end of the sermon, Rob and I both fought tears. The pastor asked the congregation to stand and close our eyes as the band played softly in the background.

God, if you're real — if that Jesus I saw on the beach is real — please show me.

I lifted my head to see a silhouette of Jesus cast in the sunlight through one of the windows. I was breathless.

"It doesn't matter what you've done, and what's been done to you," the preacher said. "You can give it to Jesus right now. He's standing here, with open arms, waiting to forgive you. Come down to the front and trade your pain for his joy."

Rob and I didn't hesitate. He hurried to one side of the altar and I went to the middle. I dropped to a fetal position on the maroon carpet. "I'm sorry, I'm so sorry," I sobbed with my face in my hands. "Forgive me. Take my life and make me a new mom, and a new person."

For the next week, I had trouble sleeping because I physically felt a dark presence hovering over me as vivid, terrifying images of my past replayed in my mind. One night I got out of bed and told the Christian housemother, Lenora, what was happening to me.

"Write a Dear John letter to your addiction," she said, handing me her personal journal and a pen.

For the next hour, my hand sped across the pages of her little book, spilling my anger in blue ink. It was raw. It was real.

"I hate you! You're not my friend!" I wrote. "You want to f***ing kill me but now I'm gonna kill you! You don't have my best interests in mind, but God does. So you will get the f*** out of my life ..."

Lenora tore my rage from her book and stuffed it in a sand art bottle, leftover from art therapy class. The women's housing was on the beach, and Lenora walked me out the back door and through the darkness to the water. The cool, gentle tide lapped over my bare feet as we looked out over the deep.

"As big as that ocean is, that's as big as God is, and you're going to give it all to him," she said. I launched the bottle, and my past, into the sea with all the force I could muster.

After I graduated from the 28-day program, I went to a Christian halfway house. Besides daily therapy and exercise, I learned to read the Bible and pray. All the while, I longed for my children, but everyone assured me I was no good to them until I got well.

When I arrived home in October, Melody and Trent jumped on me with the tightest, longest bear hugs! We went straight to a costume Harvest Party at Chase's church. It was like an indoor fair in the gymnasium with a moon bounce, pony rides and game booths. Chase never took his eyes off me as I played with the kids. Afterward, he walked me to the car.

"I see something different about you," he said. "Will you date me again? Can we just get to know each other again?" I could see he'd changed, too.

Over the next few months, we went on dates and family outings and attended church together. By February, we were engaged and in premarital counseling with our pastor. Jesus had done so much already to restore our lives! And now, we had to let him help us face truth head-on so we could trust each other again.

So we sat on a blanket in my living room one night and asked each other the lingering questions. Honest answers ripped the Band Aids off our knees exposing grotesque, excruciating wounds. I left the room to vomit several times. Chase did the same. Ultimately, the open air healed the wounds and let us start over, clean. We'd thrown our sins in the ocean for Jesus — and each other — to forgive.

We married in June 2000 and the first year was wonderful. But the next year, we started skipping church. I stopped praying and reading my Bible. We started going out for drinks with friends.

I had an affair with a guy I met at the bar and started snorting coke with him. Then, I dabbled with the crack pipe again. The further I got from the new life God had given me, the more I wanted it back. My relapse lasted several months, until I turned to Chase for help in August 2001. He was furious! I went back to the Florida rehab and in the meantime, Chase sold my car, planned a divorce and took custody of the kids.

The most Chase would offer me was to pray briefly for me five times a day, and I did the same for him. In time, God helped Chase forgive me and I worked hard to win back his trust. It was no easy road, and would not have happened with out God's help.

In 2002, we bought a house in Atglen and became a family for good. We've since been blessed with twin daughters! We have good jobs and serve in our church, Freedom Life Christian Center, counseling struggling couples. God is still doing for others what he's done for us, and we're so thankful to be part of it!

I deserve to be dead or in jail. I deserve to have lost my mental faculties. I deserve to have given birth to a drug-addicted, handicapped baby. I deserve to have lost my children and any hope of true love. I deserve to be alone.

But God didn't give me what I deserve. He gave me Jesus, and Jesus forgave me! He let the old Callie die, and made me into a whole new person. He did the same for Chase, too. God did the impossible, teaching us to forgive each other like he has forgiven us. I see Jesus every day in my kind, loving husband and precious children.

Ezekiel 36:26 promises, "I will give you a new heart and put a new spirit in you ..." and that's what he did for us! Jesus forgave my past, healed my heart, and loves me more than any man ever could. He took my past and gave me joy! And for that, I pursue life with him harder than I ever pursued a high.

Toy Story
Michael's Back Story

"Okay, here's what we're gonna do," I told a kid I knew as we stood outside Sears. I couldn't call my fellow seventh-grader a friend, because I had none. No one cared about me, and I didn't care about anyone else.

"We're gonna go in, grab one thing and get out of there. Hit and run, man," I said.

"Cool. What are you gonna get?" he asked.

"I'm going for the Aerialbots," I said. Aerialbots was a box set of five jet plane Transformers that could be assembled into one giant robot, Superion. In 1985, it was the ultimate new toy.

"Just make sure what you pick is worth it. They have cameras and security so the only way to do this is fast. Get it?" I advised.

"Yeah, let's do this," he said as we walked through the doors.

I went straight for the toy department with my backpack. After looking both ways for security, I snatched the 24-inch square gift set off the shelf, ripped it open and dumped my new playmates in. There was Silverbolt, the Concorde jet; Skydive, the F-16 Fighting Falcon; Fireflight, an F-4 Phantom II; Slingshot, the AV-8B Harrier II; and Air Raid, the F-15 Eagle. I grabbed the sticker set and instructions out of the box, zipped up my backpack and hurried to the sporting goods department. I lifted a preassembled skateboard and made for the exit with my protégé on my heels.

I dropped the skateboard on the asphalt parking lot and skated off just as two security guards tackled the other kid. I only got away because I had wheels and they were busy busting him.

It wasn't my first hit. I had mastered stealing from other stores, like Kmart. They sold appliances then and I would squeeze between two refrigerators, rip my prize out of its packaging and stuff it in my pants. Then, I would walk out free and clear.

I had no remorse — not even when I stole from a 4-year-old boy. He lived in the apartment next to us when I was 8, and sometimes I'd hang out with him because he had the best toys — and lots of them! But not for long. I swiped the spare key off his kitchen counter one day and returned with a box when no one was home. I packed every one of his toys into that box: Matchbox and Hot Wheels cars, action figures, Fisher Price toddler toys and more. Like the *Grinch Who Stole Christmas*, I didn't leave a single one behind.

I hid the box under the bed I shared with my single mother in our one-bedroom apartment. Eventually she found them and freaked out. "Where did these toys come from?" she demanded, cussing at me as usual.

As I mastered my thievery, I crafted lies. I told her I found them or that I traded toys with another kid. My classic line was that a kid at school got duplicates for his birthday and gave me one.

We were on welfare and could never afford the toys I stole. At Christmas, Mom could only offer me a dollar store toy or two. If she was able to spend $20, it was a very merry Christmas morning. But when I was 9, one of her boyfriends gave me the best gift ever: the G.I. Joe Killer W.H.A.L.E.! The hovercraft came with the Cutter action figure, elevating cannons, rotating machine guns and six depth charges. Not only was it beyond anything we could afford, it was too big to steal. This was the jackpot!

I went to 15 schools by the end of junior high so I was always the new kid to ignore or tease. But action figures and skateboards didn't judge me by my outgrown clothes or need of a haircut.

My mother was 15 when she gave birth to me in Sacramento, California in 1974. My father was also a teenager and, depending on whose side of the story you believe, I was conceived either by a one-night stand or rape. A few weeks after I was born, my mother snapped due to ongoing sexual abuse by her father and went after him with a knife. As a result, the state put me in foster care. When I was 2 ½, my mother married to show the court that she had a stable home in order to regain custody. It worked and she divorced just weeks after I was home.

She may have loved me, but she didn't pay much attention to me. She often slept until noon because she had a drug problem. At 4 years old, I got myself up each morning, fixed a bowl of generic, cardboard-flavored puff cereal, and caught the bus to preschool. By the time I was 10, I would walk, skateboard or bicycle about five miles through traffic to the mall and other shopping centers to take what I wanted.

"Step right up! You Sir, you look like a winner," the carnival man beckoned, holding out a softball for my dad. It was my sixth birthday and the first time I remember meeting my dad.

"Three out of five gets you a small, and five gets you a medium," said the man as I gazed at the wall of stuffed animals behind him.

Dad pulled cash from his pocket and snatched off a couple of bills for the carnie who laid out the balls in front of him. "Sure, let's get one for the kid. It's his birthday."

Wham! The stacked milk bottles toppled over. Wham! They fell again. And again. He went five for five.

"What do you want?" he looked down at me.

"That one!" I pointed to a 12-inch stuffed dinosaur that mimicked Dino from the *Flintstones* cartoon.

I saw my father once in a while after that, but mostly I waited on the apartment stairs, watching for his car that never came. My mother tells me that after one of these instances, I set a fire in the apartment complex. But, as with much of my angry childhood, I don't remember. I set a second apartment fire when I was 8, just to

66

see how fast the firemen would arrive. I was an ill-tempered terror, desperate for attention and love, yet incapable of connecting emotionally with another human being. Empathy and remorse were just not in my DNA.

The same year, I did an experiment to see if even my mother noticed me. I hid in the electrical room of the apartment complex for most of the day. Finally, I snuck back into the apartment and hid behind a coffee table connecting the couches in the corner.

"I don't know where he is," my mom sobbed on the phone. "Are you sure he's not over there?"

She called everyone she could think of. When she left the room, I crawled out of hiding and sat on the couch, just waiting for her to walk by and *not* notice me. But notice me she did!

"You little ..." she laid into me with a barrage of profanity. "Where have you been?! Who do you think you are disappearing like that?"

Mom was stuck in minimum wage retail and fast food jobs and wanted something better, so when I was in second grade, she joined the Navy. She headed for basic training in Orlando, and I was dropped off to live in a desert campground on the fringe of Las Vegas with her father and stepmother. Our home was a brown and white, short-chassis Winnebago the size of a conversion van. At night, I climbed into the bunk above the cab, pulled the little curtain shut and slept with my Dino.

Midway through that second grade school year, my grandfather sent me to live with my aunt in San Diego. Eventually, my mother was stationed there and we moved into an apartment next door to my aunt.

Within six months, my mother's ship was called to tour the West Pacific. I'd been a handful for my grandparents and my aunt the first time around, so they didn't want me back. With no one else to take custody of me, my mother was discharged and we went on welfare. We moved often, usually around the San Diego area.

Mom had a lot of men in and out of her life; some were live-ins. When I was 11, she dated a drug dealer with three kids in high school and one day, they were sitting around smoking weed and offered me some. I acted real goofy and made them laugh. The attention from these older cool kids was thrilling, so I smoked it with them whenever they offered.

"Where can I get my own pipe?" I asked the oldest boy, 17.

He took me inside an adult bookstore where I bought my first pipe and I started getting my own pot from him.

One day when I was halfway into sixth grade, my mom broke the news. "I'm trying to get back in the Navy so you're going up state to live with your dad," she said. "He's going to pick you up and take you to Disneyland on the way there."

Disneyland? Cool! I heard Dad had a nice house and a good job working in his family's business. Life was about to get real good.

This time Dad did show, pulling up in his new white Monte Carlo SS with gray velour interior. I'd never been in a new vehicle. I breathed deep through my nostrils, taking in a new car scent for the very first time. Fascinated, I played with the button that made the power windows go up and down. This was way better than mom's 1980 Ford LTD with ratty interior and no hubcaps.

But the good life stopped with the car and Disneyland.

Dad was general manager of the multi-million dollar diesel truck dealership his father started. His younger brother was the salesman and my grandfather was gradually moving toward part-time to let his sons take over.

I moved into a nice house with Dad, his wife and my half-sister. I took Dad's last name and met his side of the family for the first time, which was awkward because I never could connect with people. In fact, to this day, the only family I'm truly close to are my wife and kids. Everyone else in my family is at arms-length or further, but I'm working on that.

Within weeks of my arrival, Dad and his wife were divorcing. We moved out and things sped downhill faster than a Matchbox on a plastic yellow track.

As with each time I moved, my clothes gave kids plenty of reasons to make fun of me. Mom took me shopping just once a year. But like any preteen boy, I grew out of my clothes before the season was over, so my pants and sleeves were too short and my shoes were too small.

"Attention Kmart shoppers, there is now a Blue Light Special in the boys' department. For the next 15 minutes, selected shirts are 50 percent off," a woman's voice would announce.

"Come on," Mom would say, ushering me to the flashing blue police-style light on a silver pole above of a rack of clearance clothing.

So here I was again — the new kid with misfit clothes — midway into sixth grade.

On the positive side, Dad got me a cat. It was the first living thing I actually loved, which is odd because I hate cats today. Dad also introduced me to man movies on TV — spaghetti westerns and Clint Eastwood flicks like *The Outlaw of Josie Wales* and *Fist Full of Dollars.*

But good times ended there.

Dad cut long lines of cocaine on the bar in our house. He drank, which tended to put him in a foul mood so the smallest offense triggered his rage. He gave me money to buy dinner while he went on benders (sometimes he was gone for days). I did what any sixth-grader would do; I bought a box of mac-n-cheese or Ramen noodles and spent the rest on candy and ice cream.

On one occasion, Dad was gone for several days so I biked a couple of miles to my great-grandfather's house. Great-Grandpa was a highly distinguished veteran and Dad respected him immensely.

"Yeah, Dad hasn't been around for a while," I told him. "I'm kinda worried."

Dad had been missing from work for days, too.

"You head home, son and I'll take care of it," he told me.

I went home and locked the door while my great-grandfather and grandfather went to find Dad in one of the bars. When they located him, they laid into him pretty good and ordered him home. Dad was angry that I'd told the person he admired, so he came home with vengeance on his mind.

Bam! Dad landed a kick to the front door, busting it open. He always reminded me of the antagonist in *The Karate Kid*, with sandy blond hair, a big ego and even bigger temper. He was even a brown belt in a martial art.

Terrified, I grabbed my cat, ran for my room and hid in an empty appliance box I'd been using for a fort. Dad stormed in, punching walls and yelling obscenities.

"Don't you *ever* go to Grandpa again!" he threatened. Then he went into the backyard and kicked in the wooden fence boards until his rage subsided.

Mom didn't get into the Navy. So at the end of the school year, I was happy to return home to her for seventh grade!

We lived in the skateboarding Mecca of San Diego where Tony Hawk was taking the sport to a whole new level. Every so often Dad sent me 50 bucks in the mail, which to me was like winning a million dollar lotto. I would head straight for the skate shop to buy a Tony Hawk deck, new trucks, wheels or other skate paraphernalia.

One day as I sat on the floor with my skateboard, my mother handed me the phone. "It's your grandfather," she said.

"Hi," I said.

"Hey, I just wanted to let you know your dad is in the hospital. He had a heart attack," Grandpa said. "He's going to be okay though."

Okay or not, I was crushed. As I bawled like a baby, I looked at my skateboard, realizing it could have been the last thing my dad ever gave me.

Dad was just 28 years old, and had been stabbed in the heart years earlier with a butterfly knife in a bar fight. His cocaine use had thrust his already weak heart into arrest.

I vowed to never touch weed, or any drug, again.

I continued to steal though and was angry all the time. I even hit my mother a few times. At the end of the school year, she decided she couldn't handle me anymore and shipped me back to my father in northern California.

In the meantime, my grandfather had given Dad an ultimatum: get clean or you're out of the family business. Dad was keeping his end of the bargain with respect to drugs, but he still drank.

Dad bought me nice clothes and other necessities, but I continued to steal. I was a pro by now. I could spot plain clothes security personnel on the spot. If they weren't around, I took what I wanted. If they were present, I taunted them. First, I followed them around the store for a while to let them know I was watching. Then, I spoke into an invisible Walkie-Talkie.

"Yeah, Joe, I've got a suspect in aisle six," I'd say into my cupped hands for effect, loud enough for them to hear me.

A few months after I moved back in with Dad, I got caught. I don't remember what I stole, but I will never forget what happened afterward.

"Hand it over," Grandpa said, pointing to my skateboard when he picked me up. The rest of the way home, he said nothing.

Grandpa was the only person in the world whom I respected. He was the only person whose approval really mattered to me, and his silence was as long as the depth of his disappointment. It was the first time I was ever sorry for what I'd done.

I never stole another thing again. Not one thing. Not ever.

I never saw my mother, except for a couple of times during high school. That was okay because I didn't want to see her either.

I didn't want anything to do with my former Blue Light Special life, constant moves and neglect. I wanted to move on.

Dad was dating his second wife, and within a year of my moving in, they married. We moved into a home they built. Our household now included my half-sister, my stepmother's two kids, and me. I was suddenly the oldest of four with another sibling on the way.

Dad was off drugs, but he still had two huge problems: drinking and rage. He was a violent, angry drunk. It was easy to set him off, and when I did, he would punch me or give me a powerful kick in the shin.

One day, when I was 14, we somehow got on the subject of God. It quickly escalated into a fierce argument.

"What do you mean God's not real? Of course he's real!" my non-practicing Catholic father shouted.

I was a freshman, so of course I knew everything, *especially* that there is no God. "You can't prove to me that there is a God because there isn't one!" I barked. I thought he would punch me again, but he didn't.

Within a week or so, my stepmother got the brunt of one of his fits. I saw him punch her in the face so hard she had to get stitches at the emergency room.

With his fledgling marriage falling apart, Dad's secretary offered a shred of hope. "Why don't you come to my church?" she invited.

Dad must have figured that, if God was real, he was the only hope for his marriage. That Sunday, Dad commanded our household to attend.

I hated it. I hated it before I got there. I hated the drive and the pews and the full-blown choir and the preacher's robe. Most of all, I hated my dad for making me go and I wanted it to show. I sat in the back with my arms crossed, scowling.

Dad dragged our family there every Sunday after that. It wasn't long before he forced me to go to teen Sunday school, and then, youth group. I spoke to no one, kept my head down, did my time and left.

My dad seemed bent on tormenting me with this church stuff and within weeks of our argument about God, he signed me up for summer youth camp. We lived 45 minutes from church, so I didn't even go to school with these kids much less talk to them. I certainly didn't want to spend a week in the Sierra Nevadas with these Bible-thumpers.

At camp, I didn't talk much to people and tried to stay under the radar. But then something unusual happened. This popular, cool-kid jock, James, asked me to hang out.

"Hey, you want to go play basketball?" he asked.

"Sure," I said, even though I had no idea how to play basketball. Having being raised by a single mom with no parenting skills I had never played sports. In fact, I was always the last kid picked for kickball and other team activities in gym.

James continued to initiate hanging out and for the first time in my life, I felt accepted. As a result, I became more comfortable with the other kids and actually developed a peer group — something I'd never experienced before! *So this is what love feels like!*

Services were held each night at camp. A band played the current Christian music like Michael W. Smith and Keith Green, which I thought was pretty good and better than listening to the robed choir at church. After the music, a youth evangelist would preach.

Midweek, the speaker ended his talk with the band playing softly behind him. I don't remember his sermon, or what he said next. But in that moment, I knew I was not just loved by my peers, but also by God.

So you are real. And you do love me. The revelation overwhelmed me.

I joined in as the preacher led us in a prayer to ask God's forgiveness for our wrongs. I sure had plenty of those! When he invited us to come forward if we wanted to know Jesus, I didn't hesitate. God was already tugging on my heart.

When I got to the edge of the little stage, someone prayed with me. For the first time in my life, I experienced hope. I'd never had dreams. But now, I sensed that God had a great future for me!

It wasn't too long after I got home from camp that Dad and my stepmother made the same decision to follow Jesus.

I went all in. I read the Bible and went to youth group and Bible studies. I joined the church volleyball and softball teams.

At that time, in California, you could get a driver permit at age 15 ½ and a license on your 16th birthday. As soon as I could drive, my Grandpa bought a 1981 Datsun King Cab pick-up for me. It was four-wheel drive, white with blue stripes and a cap on the back. I drove it to church every time there was something going on.

Having friends at church gave me the confidence to make friends at school, too. I acted in school plays and had the lead role in *Our Town*.

Junior year, I joined the youth choir. I auditioned for a solo in our church musical, *Friends: Featuring the Music of Michael W. Smith*. I was turned down but sang in the regular choir. Also during junior year, I went on a 10-day mission trip to Mexicali, Mexico.

In my senior year, I joined a small touring group within the school choir called the Meister Singers as a tenor. We sang Renaissance music in costume; I wore puffy sleeves, a skirt, tights and a hat with a feather in it!

Because I felt loved, I was finally able to connect with my peers. And because I stayed in one place throughout high school, I was able to maintain those relationships and explore my interests. By the time I graduated, I had real friends.

When I was 17, my aunt addressed my dramatic turnaround.

"I was certain you'd be dead or in prison by 16," she admitted. "What changed?"

"Jesus," I said, smiling.

It was near the end of senior year and I had been accepted to study business at Eastern University in St. Davids, Pennsylvania. I was all about making money; I was not going to do without like I did with my mom.

I worked at the family dealership then. I cleaned toilets, pulled weeds, picked people up at the airport, ran parts, washed tractor-trailers and anything else I was asked to do.

One day, I was sudsing up a huge Kenworth truck when I started dreaming — well, sort of, because I was wide-awake! In this surreal vision, I saw people sitting on the grass and blankets on a hillside. They faced a stage rigged up for an outdoor concert, but there was absolutely no sound. I saw a person on stage at the mic — and it was me! Suddenly, I was standing next to the Dream Me on stage. My conscious self walked up to my dream self on the stage and looked up, down and all around.

"What the heck is going on?" I asked.

Just like that, ambient noise kicked in as if a mute button were released. Dream Me addressed the audience through the mic.

"Jesus saves," he said, and walked off stage as the crowd cheered.

The bizarre experience ended abruptly and I was staring at the soapy truck again, sponge in hand. I felt a very deep "knowing" that God wanted me in music and I decided to change my major to music.

I shared the experience with no one, but told my school choir director that I planned to study music now.

"What do I need to do to know going in?" I asked. I couldn't even read music!

"Well, it doesn't really work that way," he said carefully. "But okay, here is what you need. You need voice lessons and you need to learn to play an instrument."

So that summer, I took voice lessons from him and piano lessons from the church musical director. At my first piano lesson, my instructor asked me to sing.

"Sing *Amazing Grace* for me," she said.

"Amazing grace how sweet the sound," I sang. "That saved a wretch like me ..."

She listened thoughtfully as I finished the song. "What happened?" she asked.

"What do you mean?"

"When you tried out for the *Friends* musical — I hate to say this — but you couldn't sing to save your life," she said. "But *that* was beautiful!"

"I don't know, I just always thought I could, so I went after it," I shrugged.

I took as many voice and piano lessons as I could that summer before driving my Datsun pick-up across the country to start school in Pennsylvania. Shortly after I arrived, I met with my advisor.

"Hi, my name is Michael," I said, shaking his hand and sitting down across from his desk. "It's very nice to meet you, but I'm going to change my major to music so I don't know that you and I have much to talk about."

"Actually, I'm the choir director. I'm handling the business department's advisement overflow," he explained. "Welcome to the program. And congratulations! Let me tell you a story," he began, leaning back in his chair.

Eastern didn't have a music program, he explained. But over the summer, someone found an original Mozart manuscript in the basement of Eastern's theological seminary in Philadelphia. The school auctioned it at Sotheby's in London and committed the proceeds to launch a music department this semester. I was the first student, arriving before they had even hired a department chair.

It hadn't occurred to me that Eastern might not have a music program. I just assumed it did because I was so sure God was leading me there. The chain of events leading to the birth of a music department began immediately after my vision. As I was preparing with lessons, God was preparing the place for me to study at Eastern.

I hadn't mastered an instrument, had little musical experience and was just learning to read music. No other college would have admitted me as a music major. But because I was already at Eastern, and there was only one other music major, they welcomed me.

It also meant personal attention from the best of the best. The department chair became my mentor and the choir director and several others held my hand through four years of study.

Junior year, I was walking past a room when I heard musicians auditioning for entrance to the program. *Man, that stinks for you,* I thought. I knew my path was not by chance. It was providential, and I was honored to become the first graduate of Eastern's music program four years later.

It was the fifth day of my sophomore year when I saw an attractive freshman brunette walking with some friends on campus.

"Hey, check her out," I told Carter. Carter had become my best friend and would ultimately be the godfather of my children. God had truly brought me a long way in relating to others. But he wasn't done with me yet.

"Oh, I met her last night," he said.

That night Carter, our friend Henry, and I were in floor seating for a concert in the campus gym when the cute brunette walked up to us. "Hey Henry, hey Carter," she said. "Can I hang with you guys? I'm bored up there with my floormates."

"Chris, this is Danielle," Carter said, inventing my alias. "Danielle, this is Chris."

"Nice to meet you," she said.

After the concert, I tried to clear up the name prank Carter played. She refused to believe my name was Michael until I pulled out my driver's license!

It was a predictable Christian concert, with several "forced fellowship" moments; the kind where the leader instructs you to find someone you don't know and tell that person three things about yourself in 30 seconds. Danielle and I leaned over to talk from three seats away each time.

"So, what year are you?" she asked.

"Sophomore," I said.

"Oh, good. So you're gonna be around for a while so I can get to know you," she said. She would call that her cheesy pick-up line.

It worked. We met later in the lobby between our adjoining dorm wings.

"I'm gonna go for a walk," she said.

"Well, you can't walk alone out there. It's dangerous," I said. That was my own cheesy line, which also worked. We walked the campus until 6 a.m., talking and telling our life stories. We were an instant item.

But a few weeks later, I had a Stupid Moment when it dawned on me that I could date around. I had confidence with people now and knew I could get dates, so I broke up with Danielle to play the field.

My waywardness only lasted about a week, when a close mutual friend knocked sense into me. "What's your problem, dude?" he asked. "You're an idiot. This girl over here adores you and you want to chase other girls?"

Danielle accepted my apology and took me back. Our courtship was intense and volatile. We wrecked our spiritual lives by sleeping together and the silliest disagreements turned into screaming matches in the dorm lobby. Ironically, the fights were often about the future we were planning together. She wanted to go to a small Pentecostal church; I wanted to go to a Baptist mega church. She wanted six kids; I wanted zero to two. She wanted a small house; I wanted a big house.

Our arguments were usually punctuated by shouting from the dorms, "Shut up, you two! It's three in the morning! Just break up already!"

When we got engaged in December 1993, Carter and Danielle's best friend tried to talk us out of it. But we were both stubborn and convinced we belonged together.

I hadn't been home to California except for one brief visit the summer after my freshman year. So Danielle and I flew out to visit my dad over Christmas break.

I can't remember what started my argument with my father, but I was shouting from the bedroom and he was shouting from the next room. I was determined to have my respect and declared, "I'm a man now! Let's go!"

In the time it takes to snap one's fingers, he was in the room, jumped over the king size bed and punched me dead in the face, knocking me down right in front of Danielle.

"Who's a man now?" he asked.

We married in June 1996 in the university chapel a month after my graduation and the end of her junior year. Danielle was eight months pregnant, a fact she hid from most people — including some of her closest friends — by wearing baggy, tomboy clothes.

Danielle's family and a handful of friends attended our wedding, but not one single member of my family came. (My father had come to my graduation though.)

The entire wedding cost $450. Danielle's friend supplied our cake and we bought the bridal bouquet at Acme. Danielle bought a pretty dress at J.C. Penney and I went to Men's Warehouse for a business suit. We didn't have a honeymoon. I landed a job as a car salesman during finals week and we moved into an apartment in Bridgeport.

When our daughter was born, she was as beautiful as her mother and I determined to give her the parenting and provision I didn't have. My dad's finances, marriage and commitment to Jesus fell apart while I was in college and I was determined not to be like him. He was on his second divorce; I said I'd have a good marriage. He beat his wife; I said I'd never hit mine. He had become a financial failure; my family and I would never do without.

But the spiritual decay that started with our neglect of Bible reading and prayer, sporadic church attendance and premarital sex had eaten away our chances for any of those things before we ever said, "I do."

Our fighting was consistent and intense as usual. All the anger of my childhood raged against my will to contain it. I hit Danielle several times that first year. Car sales didn't make ends meet and a local church paid our rent one month. By September, I quit and took a job selling cellular phones.

I didn't know how to care for somebody else, much less nurture and provide for a family. I'd let loose the spiritual moorings of a church family, Bible reading and prayer and now I was drifting out with the tide, away from Jesus. And without him, I am basically a monster.

Danielle took an internship in social work during her senior year where she found another guy to meet her emotional needs. I noticed she spent an increasing amount of time with him, even outside the office, so I started following her around. One night, I waited in the cemetery across the street from our apartment for her to come home. Would she take the train home like she said, or would someone drop her off?

Her coworker's car pulled in and parked. They sat in the car talking for at least 15 minutes before Danielle called it a night. I went storming into the apartment.

"What do you think your doing? Don't tell me there's nothing going on!"

"There's not! But what do you care?"

"You said you were taking the train home! You spent too much time parked in that car. You're sleeping with him, I know it!"

She wasn't though — at least, not yet.

I grabbed my keys, stormed out of the apartment and landed crying on Carter's doorstep in Northeast Philly at about one o'clock in the morning.

Over the next few hours, my sobs of, "I don't know what I'm gonna do," turned into, "I'm gonna leave her because she's gonna cheat on me!" A while longer, and I had a rational thought. *Men cheat because they just want booty. Women look for emotional support outside the marriage when they don't get it at home. So this is my fault.*

Danielle was looking for someone to love her because I wasn't loving her! I drove home at 5 a.m. and crawled into bed with my wife.

"We're gonna make this work," I whispered, stroking her long, dark brown hair. "I'll take responsibility to meet your needs. And we have to find a church home if we're going to make it."

We had always agreed that the word "divorce" would never be spoken in our home. I watched my father and his two wives throw it at each other like darts during fights. It's no wonder their marriages failed.

We decided to go the next step and start saying, "We're going to make it, and we are going to have a great marriage," even on the toughest of days. And we would need God's help to do so.

It was early in 1998 when we visited a new church in our area and immediately felt at home. It felt like my week at summer camp all over again; I felt loved. I'd never stopped believing in Jesus or that he loved me. I just hadn't felt it in a long time because of all the junk in my life. I'd been having sex with my girlfriend before we married, I was inconsistent in church attendance and I'd been more focused on studying music than studying my Bible. Living without a moral compass left me struggling to make ends meet and be a decent husband and father.

I knew this church was the place Jesus would help me turn things around.

Not long after we started attending, Pastor Jerry heard me singing as I stood in the pew behind him during worship.

"You have to join our worship team," he insisted.

"Thanks, Pastor, but no. You don't want me up there. I'm just now getting my spiritual life back together and trying to repair my broken marriage," I said. But six months later, I finally agreed to sing backup vocals.

This wasn't what I'd aspired to do when I went to Eastern. I always wanted to be a singer and songwriter and definitely not a worship leader. Until this point, I though worship was a joke. I was all about everything Christian, except the worship music at church. I thought people who were into it were just fooling themselves with a religious activity. But at this church, I began to see the freedom and life there is in genuine musical worship.

We moved to Wayne, which happened to be just a few miles from Pastor Jerry's home, where he regularly invited us to hang out with him on his deck. He became a true father to me and I would ask him questions about how to handle situations in my life. He gave me books like *The Five Love Languages*, which gave me tools to improve my marriage. I'd always read business books because I knew if I grew in business, I'd make more money. Now, I was trying to grow spiritually to improve my relationship with God, my wife and my family, which now included our second daughter, born in 1999.

I had started writing songs with Pastor Jerry's son, who was the worship leader. I had the voice and he had the guitar talent and we wrote together well. We were going to make the big time together.

But in 1999, he announced that in a matter of weeks, he was quitting to go to Christ for the Nations Institute to study. My dreams were shattered and I cried as much as I did when I thought Danielle was going to cheat on me.

Then Pastor Jerry asked me to be the worship leader. I prayed about it and accepted — not because I wanted to, but because there was a need that I was capable of filling.

I was terrible! The only songs I could play on guitar were the ones I'd written, but leading people in worship requires you to play an instrument, unless you have a really strong band. I still have some VHS tapes of me trying to lead and every now and then we pop them in the VCR and laugh. I had a long way to go!

I practiced two hours a night just to prepare for Sunday's set list, read all the books I could about worship and went to some conferences. *God, if you want me to do this, I'm going to learn everything I can about genuine worship.*

One night in 2000, I was playing in a Christian coffee house on Route 113 in Phoenixville with my band. We were playing contemporary Christian music and songs we'd written to an audience that consisted of Pastor Jerry, his family and my wife and kids. Talk about discouraging! This was supposed to be my path to the dream! It was supposed to lead me to that moment I saw in the vision of myself on a concert stage.

As I walked around the parking lot pondering this I prayed. *God, what do you want me to do?*

He answered in that moment with the realization that music was never about Jesus for me, it was about my own dreams of success. God wanted me in music to change lives. Worship music couldn't be about me for that to happen.

You're right, God. I'm sorry. I guess I have to be transparent and genuine in my worship for it to bring others closer to you. I will never play anything but worship music again.

Of course, I wasn't knocking Christian pop music. I just realized it was never my calling. My dream now was full-time ministry.

By stepping up simply to meet the need for a worship leader at church, I had unknowingly stepped through the door to God's plan for my life!

In 2004, a church in Paoli asked me to lead worship for a contemporary service on Sunday nights. I accepted the paid position and put together a full band from talent in their congregation. Three hundred people showed up the first night, but attendance dwindled to 50 within six months. In February 2006, a new pastor came on board and the contemporary service was canceled.

During that time we continued to attend our church and I remained the worship leader there. The job in Paoli boosted our income just enough to buy a home in Honey Brook, a solid 45 minutes from both my church and my day job in the cellular business.

After the contemporary service was cancelled I was disillusioned again. *God, I thought you were leading me into full-time ministry and that this was my break. What is up with that? Where do you want me, God? Where is my opportunity?*

The answer was, *Right here where you are. Be faithful here and I will take you further when it's time.* So I continued in my volunteer role at my home church.

"I think it's time to move on," Danielle told me about a year later. "Our kids will be teenagers soon and they need to be part of a youth group." Our eldest was 11 and about to enter junior high and our youngest was 9. Our church had only a small core of families and the majority of the members were transient students from nearby colleges.

"Yeah, I know. I've been feeling the same way," I said.

I didn't know how to approach Pastor Jerry, who had become a father to me. I didn't want to disappoint or hurt him. After all, it wasn't like I was leaving to take a staff position somewhere. Yet

Pastor Jerry had taught me that my family comes first and if I fail them, I will fail in ministry.

We sat at the table on his back deck having iced tea when we broke the news.

"Yes, I sensed that too," he said. "I have peace about it. I was wondering when you were going to come to me."

What a relief! He gave us his blessing for our plan to visit other churches once a month until we found the right fit. I had already been training another worship leader and he could certainly handle things.

I hoped to find a church that needed a worship leader, but my first priority was finding a good youth program for our daughters. A customer at work invited me to check out his church in Coatesville, which was much closer to our home.

The people seemed nice, the worship was decent and they had a youth program. They didn't need a worship leader, but everything else seemed to fit and we decided to return the next month.

On our second visit, the worship leader announced she was taking a one-year sabbatical to travel with a band overseas. I put in my resume and was hired as an interim worship leader. Over the next 15 months we were able to have an impact, taking their worship team to the next level. Eventually, we decided the church was not the right fit for our family. For six months, we visited others looking for a new home.

In December 2008, we visited Freedom Life Christian Center in Christiana and it was anything but traditional. It was progressive in everything from worship music to a black stage, professional lighting and an excellent sound system. People wore jeans — even Pastor Sam, who preached without a pulpit, sitting on a stool. We returned once more during the winter, and again on Palm Sunday.

We sat in the second row, behind the youth pastor. Just like Pastor Jerry had done, Pastor Jake heard me singing behind him.

During the greeting time, he shook my hand and said, "What's your story? You can really sing, man."

In that 30-second window, I introduced myself and Pastor Jake asked me to lead youth worship.

"No, thanks, man. But I will pray about it," I replied.

"Okay, but let's meet for lunch this week," he said.

On Good Friday, I was shaving to meet Pastor Jake for lunch and the phone rang.

"Hello, Michael," the pastor of a large church in the area said. I had sent my resume to him because they had a full-time opening for a worship leader. "I'd like to offer you the position."

It was the call I had waited for all these years.

In that moment, I knew what God wanted me to do. I knew deep in my heart, just like I knew I was called to music as I washed the tractor-trailer years earlier.

"I'm so sorry, Pastor," I said. "But I've found something else. I wish you well in your search."

I met Pastor Jake at Chili's in Parkesburg and told him I'd lead worship for youth. "I'll do whatever you want me to do," I said. "I'll clean toilets if you want me to. God is calling me to be faithful here."

Leading teenagers in worship was way out of my comfort zone, but it's one of the most rewarding things I've ever done. Since then, I've started leading a two-year certificate program in Biblical Studies and will soon be the campus pastor at a Freedom Life satellite campus.

I've come to the realization that the whole time I wanted to be in full-time ministry, I already *was* in full-time ministry. God has progressively prepared me for each new step in this journey.

I can honestly say that today that I am closer to Jesus than I have ever been. My passion isn't a selfish ambition anymore, but reaching out to bring people close to God so he can change their lives like he has changed mine.

I don't steal toys anymore, but I am building a collection of vintage toys that were once my only friends in childhood. They remind me of where I've been, and where I am now. I can buy them because God lifted me out of poverty and a life of theft and deception. My life isn't about what I can take anymore. It's about what I can give.

Arms Open Wide
Freda Saunders' Back Story

"Freda, it's time to go get your bath," Mom said. At 8 years old, that was certainly something I could handle myself.

I poured more than a few drops of Mr. Bubble under the faucet as it gushed water into the bathtub at just the right temperature. Then I stepped into the mountainous froth and lowered myself into the warmth below.

I cupped my hands to scoop some of the soapy meringue, heaved a burst of breath at it and watched it flurry over the other floating mountains. The bubbles were airy and warm, unlike the December snow we expected any day.

I'd barely started washing when Mom came in and sat on the side of the bathtub. "Honey, what would you do if your dad died?" she asked matter-of-factly.

"I'd kill myself," I shot back, soaping up the washrag. *What a ridiculous thing to ask! Why would she ask me that?*

She paused. "Honey, your dad died."

Like a stealth alligator sliding into the river, I sank my body under the froth until my hair was soaked and water lapped over my face.

She's kidding. It's some cruel joke and he's at his apartment above Harry's Bar. But Mom wouldn't joke about this.

If it's true, I'm never coming up for air.

My mother often pressed my father to marry her. The values of her religious upbringing and Christian college weighed heavy on her conscience. She gave birth to me out of wedlock in 1978 and she wanted to make things "right with God."

Dad had been married before and had two children: a son, Tim, who is 14 years older than me; and a daughter, Tammy, who is 11 years older than me. Mom was also married previously and had two daughters: Beth, who is 11 years older than me; and Carolyn, who is 10 years older than me.

Fearing another failed marriage, Dad refused to tie the knot with my mother. His predictions came true when I was 4 years old and Mom threw him out because of his chronic drinking.

Dad's best friend owned Harry's Hot Dogs in Sadsburyville, Pennsylvania, and rented the apartment above the store to Dad. I looked forward to Saturday afternoons when my father would pick me up at the twin home in Parkesburg where I lived with my mother and grandmother. He was always glad to see me, too.

"Hey, Stinker!" he'd grin, opening his arms to wrap me in a bear hug.

We had a Saturday routine. Our first stop was the Polish Club in Coatesville where my father had a few drinks and bantered with the afternoon regulars. Next, we drove to Jamesway or Kmart in Thorndale where I had my pick of any one toy I wanted. Our final destination was the pub at Harry's.

Of course, I was the only kid in the bar, so Dad's friends gave me quarters to play a hockey arcade game that I enjoyed. They weren't trying to get rid of me. They just knew I liked the game.

Sometimes I'd climb the barstool next to my dad.

"Another soda for me, Harry, and one for Stinker here," Dad would say, putting his hand on my shoulder.

Fizz sparkled off my ice-cold drink and tickled my nose on my first sips. Dad's beverage reached my nose too, but not with odorless fizz.

"Hey, that's not soda!" I said on more than one occasion.

"Sure it is! Just like yours," he'd say as I glimpsed him winking at Harry.

When it was time to go, Dad put his arm around my shoulders and gave me a squeeze. "C'mon, Stinker," he'd say cheerfully.

When I was 8 years old, we skipped a few visits because Dad was in the hospital. When I thought he was home, I called to tell him that I missed him and hoped he felt better. There was no answer.

I knew where he was when he wasn't home, though, so I called Harry at the bar.

"Hi, this is Freda," I announced in my soft, small voice. "Can I talk to my Dad?"

I could hear the clang of glasses and muffled voices from the pub, but Harry was silent for what seemed an eternity.

"He's not here," he sighed, a little annoyed.

"Okay, thanks anyway. If you see him, can you tell him I called?" I asked.

"Sure."

Harry knew Dad was dead. Everyone knew Dad was dead. Harry was caught off guard that *I* didn't know Dad was dead. It was at least a week before Mom broke the news to me in the bathtub. Like Harry, she just didn't know what to say.

She finally got it over with and now here I was, hiding under Mr. Bubble. When I emerged, Mom was gone. I dried off, put my warm flannel pajamas on and Mom tucked me into bed without mentioning Dad again until breakfast. I cried myself to sleep, and woke up crying the next morning.

I shuffled downstairs to the living room where my tearful sister, Beth, was sitting on the sofa. I dropped to my knees and collapsed my body onto the coffee table, sobbing. Beth came to my side and gently rubbed her hand on my back in silence.

For days, our household — which consisted of my great-grandmother, grandmother, mother, Beth and me — shared tears but few words. At last, Mom fumbled to tell me what happened.

"You know Dad was very sick. The doctors did everything they could," she said.

Close family gathered at my house before the funeral, which I later learned had been postponed for an autopsy. I waited in the living room with my 6 year-old cousin, both of us adorned in black dresses.

"Why did your dad shoot himself?" she asked innocently.

"He didn't shoot himself, he was sick," I said, annoyed that she didn't know what happened.

"No, I heard my mom say he had a gun in his room and he shot himself," she corrected.

"No he didn't! He was sick!" Now I was mad! How could she say such a thing?!

"Yuh, huh! I'm gonna ask mom!" she bounded up the wooden stairs with me on her heels, and burst in the bedroom where my aunt was getting ready with some other family members.

"Tell Freda her dad shot himself with a gun! She's lying!" my younger cousin demanded, breathless.

"No! He was sick!" I screamed.

The room went silent for a few long seconds.

"Shhh! Not now, girls," one of our relatives said. "Stop fighting and get ready to go. We're leaving in a few minutes."

After the funeral, I sat on the bottom bunk bed in my room, kicked off my dress shoes and stared blankly at the posters of Rainbow Brite and Care Bears taped to my creamy yellow walls. Mom came in, sat next to me and stared at the walls, too.

"You and your cousin were *both* right," she said matter-of-factly. "Dad had something called scerosis of the liver because he drank so much. The doctors told him it was so bad that he only had six months to a year left to live."

She took a deep breath, exhaling her next words.

"He couldn't handle that so he decided to take his own life."

I was speechless as we sat quietly for a minute or so and then Mom left the room. The anger switch flipped on inside of me.

How could you do this, Dad?! Why couldn't you stay with me for the time you had left?! I fumed at his abandonment.

How could you do this, God?! Why would you take my dad from me?! I raged inside. God must have abandoned me, too.

"Everywhere I go, I see your face through the crowd," Beth sang the current (1986) Christian hit by Amy Grant as she tidied the living room. "Everywhere I go, I hear your voice clear and loud ...," she swayed her body to the song's playful reggae rhythm in her head.

I plopped down on the sofa with an armful of Barbie dolls and their accessories.

"Hey, Freda, I want to tell you something," Beth sat down at the opposite end of the sofa and hugged a throw pillow.

"I know you miss your Dad, but you know, God wants to be your Daddy," she meant well, but it wasn't the first time she had said this in the months since he passed away. Determined to stay mad, I was irritated by her good intentions.

"I don't want him to be my daddy. I want my real daddy," I smarted back, pulling a gold evening dress over Barbie's perfect blonde hair. Besides, what did God care? God wasn't around to call me Stinker, take me to Jamesway or give me bear hugs and broad smiles.

Mom was religious, too. She faithfully took our family of women to Victory Chapel in Christiana on Sunday mornings and Wednesday nights. She put me on the church bus to Vacation Bible School each summer. Puppets and nice ladies with felt boards taught me Bible stories in Sunday school. We even had Bible studies in our home.

Dad was a non-practicing Catholic and religion was a sharp debate between Mom and him, even after they separated. Dad would complain to me about Mom's Pentecostal church.

"You know they roll up and down the aisles over there," he said. "Your mother better not drink the water or they'll have her handling snakes!" Of course there was no truth to his digs.

Mom considered Dad's Catholic roots fair game for bashing, too. "They think they can live like the devil all week and say a few Hail Mary prayers and they're going to Heaven," she said. "And praying to those saints, well, that's just idolatry! So he's got no room to criticize."

If rules reflected Mom's spiritual devotion, she had a first class ticket to Heaven. No Smurfs — they were witchcraft. No non-Christian music — it filled one's head with rebellious thoughts. Even some PG movies were off limits.

By the time I entered Octorara Middle School in sixth grade, I was watching music videos at my friend's house on MTV and jamming to Metallica, Guns 'n' Roses, The Fat Boys and Yo-Yo on the school bus. I just wanted to be *me* — or at least breathe enough to figure out who "me" was.

Mom caught me with the music from time to time and eventually she gave up the fight. Posters of Kirk Cameron and boy bands replaced Rainbow Brite on my bedroom walls.

She did not, however, give up her frequent lectures on sex. The message was clear: sex is disgusting and, outside of marriage, it's a sin. She wasn't blind to my becoming "boy crazy" and she feared the worst.

By the end of eighth grade, I was obsessed with Rob, a sophomore who lived down the street and wouldn't give me the time of day. Yet I was convinced he would fall in love with me and we'd get married!

That summer, another boy, Brian, cruised his bike up and down the sidewalk while I sat on the house steps with my friend. "He's cute," I leaned over and told her.

"Hey, you! Freda said you're cute!" she shouted.

He sharply jerked the handles of his BMX bike, swung the rear wheel around and peddled back.

Brian lived a couple of blocks over and was already in high school. We soon started "going out," shooting pool at his house and occasionally holding hands. I broke up with him when friends told me Rob was jealous and wanted to go out with me.

From the start, it was clear Rob wasn't interested in pool or holding hands. Our daily make-out sessions at my friend's house sent my emotions and hormones sailing. Rob wanted me! He would be mine and I would be his! By offering my body to him, I would have his heart forever! Within a week, I withheld nothing and he quenched my deep thirst for love.

We continued to have sex for several weeks, but from the day I lost my virginity to him at 13 years old, he would either ignore me or pick fights. Then he dumped me.

I gave you everything! I burned inside. *We were meant to be together! How could you do this to me?!*

Dad, God and now Rob had left me.

Rob and I were off-and-on throughout the summer. Anytime he heard I was interested in someone else, he sweet-talked me and we were right back in the same cycle of sex, anger and rejection.

In one of our "off again" stages, I briefly went out with another boy, Jason. A few weeks before the beginning of freshman year, a girl who liked him started a rumor that spread like flames on a gasoline trail: Freda had sex with Jason and three other boys together! By the first day of school everyone heard it.

It was totally not true! But it didn't matter, the damage was done and no matter how much I denied it, my peers didn't believe me. My reputation was destroyed. If I asked a boy in class for a pencil, suddenly the whole school thought I was sleeping with him.

I'm ruined. They all think I'm a slut and no one will want me.

I wished I could end it all. I couldn't pull a trigger like Dad because I didn't have a gun but I sure wished I could. I found something else to numb the relentless sting of rejection instead.

A few shameful months had passed when some girls welcomed me into their circle. They stuck up for me when others repeated the rumor or said things to my face in the lunchroom.

One night, a few of my new friends and I hovered in the shadows outside the Old Town Deli in Parkesburg where they sold carryout. An old man we knew from the neighborhood strolled toward the door. "Hey, can you hook us up?" one of the girls asked.

"What you want?" he said.

"Mad Dog," she replied, handing him a few bucks. Moments later he returned and handed her a bottle of Red Grape MD 20/20 (fortified wine) in a paper bag. It was nasty but cheap and, at 18 proof, the bum liquor got us feeling pretty good.

We never had trouble getting people to buy alcohol for us. All we had to do was wait outside Old Town or The Arms and ask the right person. I hated the taste of beer, but pretty soon I could choke down a 40-ounce malt liquor by myself because the buzz was worth it.

My friend Heather's father grew marijuana and she started stealing it from him. I had smoked my first joint when I was 12, and only a few times since. But as my friends smoked it more often, so did I.

One day a relative knocked on my open bedroom door. "Hey, you want to try something?" he said, holding up a tiny, clear bag of white powder.

"Sure," I said. I was always up for trying a new kind of high so my adrenaline surged as he tapped some of the coke onto my dresser and scraped it into lines with his driver's license. I observed carefully what to do as he snorted up a line using a rolled dollar bill for a straw. Then it was my turn.

I inhaled a line in one lone snort, felt it's bitterness in the back of my throat and then ... what a rush! My body pulsed with energy and my spirit soared with new confidence. My words tried to keep up with my accelerating thoughts but I couldn't get them out fast enough! We did a couple more lines and I was disappointed when it was gone.

My boyfriend, Kevin, came over and my nonstop chatter and nervous energy revealed what I had been doing. Kevin was the latest in a string of boyfriends I had during freshman year. Again and again, I gave myself away, each time holding out hope that this was The One who would satisfy my craving for love and never leave. *Sex is what he wants so sex will make him stay*, I reasoned. But no matter how much I gave, or didn't give, they ultimately rejected me. *Why can't I find a serious boyfriend like other girls?* I wondered. *Why don't they love me?*

"What are you on? Coke? Crack?" Kevin demanded my confession. "You know I don't want you doing that stuff. I won't hit a girl, but I'll get Janice to beat you up," he threatened. Janice was obese, mean and would do anything for Kevin. He threatened me with her often and I had good reason to be terrified.

I didn't do coke again for a long time, but not because of Kevin's threats. The only thing stopping me was that I didn't have access to it. My friends smoked pot and drank, but didn't mess with cocaine.

"You have a pretty smile," said Chris, a senior, as he leaned against the locker next to mine. "Here, let me get that for you," he held my books while I turned the combination lock and opened the metal door.

Chris was sweet and paid a lot of attention to me lately — something I enjoyed. It was obvious he liked me, but I was stuck with Kevin who threatened beatings by Janice if I broke up with him.

"You let me take care of that," Chris said, with a tender touch to my chin. He helped me call it quits with Kevin and we started going out.

Chris had been talking with a recruiter and planned to start a military career after graduation. "I love you, Freda," he said at the end of the first official week of our relationship. "I want to get married and have kids with you. I'll be stationed in Hawaii and we can be together in paradise."

This is it. This is The One! My heart pounded.

"I love you too," I said, surrendering my heart one more time.

Several weeks later, the little birdies started singing in my ear. "I heard Chris stays with a girl in Coatesville," a schoolmate told me.

Then another person ratted Chris out. "Yo, Freda, Chris is messin' with this girl Rita." Then another report came. And another.

This couldn't be happening again. He said he loved me! He wanted a family together. It just couldn't be true!

"Who's Rita?" I demanded in the hall before school.

"What?" he asked.

"Rita! The girl from Coatesville people say you're messing around with."

"Aww, they're just getting your name mixed up. You know, Freda, Rita ... kinda sounds the same, don't it?" I reluctantly bought into his explanations for almost three months until the truth punched me hard in the jaw.

"Hello," I answered the kitchen phone.

"Are you going out with Chris?" a female voice demanded.

"Yeah, he's my boyfriend. Who is this?" I was puzzled.

"Rita. And I'm coming to Parkesburg to kick your sorry a**! He's mine and you better stop messin' with him!" she shouted into the receiver.

Now, I was mad. "Okay, then! I'm at house number 718! You better get here quick so I can kick *your* a** all the way back to Coatesville!"

Why does this keep happening to me! I wished I could sink under the bubbles again.

In spite of his denial and sweet-talk, I called it quits with Chris and moped around the house, depressed at yet another rejection. I was moody, tearful and sometimes short with my mom and grandmother. My stomach growled all day because I couldn't keep food down. At just 14, I knew what was happening even before I missed my period.

A pink "plus" sign appeared at the end of the plastic stick I bought at Longenecker's Pharmacy in town. *Maybe this will make him stay. He wants a family ...* With the stick still in hand, I called Chris.

"Oh, my gosh. Oh, my gosh," he said to his buddy who was with him. "She's pregnant!" Chris was excited about it, but he certainly shouldn't have been surprised. He had often talked me out of birth control because he wanted to have a baby together.

"Freda, I miss you. I'm done with Rita and you're the one I want, baby," he baited me and set the hook to reel me in to his boat. "Be with me again and let's have a family." I gave in to Mr. Smooth Talker and we got back together.

Heather's mom drove me to Planned Parenthood for a blood test and official confirmation of my condition. Unlike Chris, the stick hadn't lied.

The next day, I crawled into bed with my mom as I sometimes did for heart-to-heart talks. I just had to say the words she dreaded most — there was no way around it.

"Mom, I'm pregnant."

She rolled over, turning her back to me, and didn't say a word. A few long minutes passed before I got up. Days later, she responded to my news in the same matter-of-fact tone way she had informed me of Dad's death.

"What do you want to do?" she asked frankly.

"I want to keep it," I said.

Her religious convictions were satisfied — I wasn't having an abortion and it seemed to me that it was all she wanted to know. She never asked if I meant to raise the baby or put him up for adoption. She never asked how I would manage motherhood at 14. I was hurt and angry.

My friend's mother called me to talk me into having an abortion. "You're too young to have a baby. You're not quite finished ninth grade! You have no idea what you are getting yourself into. Honey, you're not playing with Barbies or baby dolls here."

This is my baby and I'm keeping it! I'm not going to kill it and I'm not going to give it away! My conviction grew deeper with every appeal.

As our little boy grew in my belly, Chris and I were on and off as usual. Sweet talk, lies, break-up. Sweet talk, sex, lies, break up ... our cycle continued. Along the way, I learned Rita was due to have his baby, too, just one month after me.

After a convincing performance showing me he was finished with Rita, Chris and I were reunited just before our son, Darion, was born in February of my sophomore year. Six weeks later, I rode the school bus to Octorara while Beth and Chris' grandmother took turns babysitting. I was a mother now, yet not even old enough for a driver's license.

Most of my senior year of high school was an "off" stage with Chris and I found someone new to love me. As a drug dealer, he also provided a way to numb the pain of rejection I carried and let loose from my adult responsibilities.

He often dropped me off at an old man's house on Zion Hill Road in Atglen where there was a party going on any time of day or night. It was a buffet of narcotics and hallucinogens where, because of my boyfriend, I dined for free.

That first snort of coke off my dresser was still vivid in my mind. I could almost taste it just thinking about it and I longed to repeat the rush. At the party house, I went straight for the nose candy, then quickly moved on to smoke it in freebase form (crack).

From the first hit, my confidence was back and all was right with the world. I loved myself and sensed a deeper connection with my friends. But the euphoria didn't last long and I had to keep hitting the pipe to avoid the hard withdrawal. Crashing was a leap from a skyscraper to kiss the pavement of depression, paranoia and fatigue. When the pipe was beat, I was on my hands and knees looking for more rock. I understood why so many people binged on it for days at a time.

I smoked it a lot, but not everyday because the drug and the guilt left me sleepless. Time after time, I came home to see Darion sleeping soundly in his crib, then I'd crawl into bed, crying.

Oh my God. I can't act like this. I can't do this. How am I supposed to be a good mother and be smoking crack? I envisioned myself landing in a less suburban crack house in Philly and feared for my son's future. *This is all God's fault,* I thought. *If God loves me, why doesn't he stop me?*

And then I was back for more.

Why am I doing this again? I was just crying about this last week, and here I am again. I had to find a way out of my cycle of shame. "And by the way, where are you, God?"

I needed to stay away from Zion Hill Road and that meant staying away from my dealer boyfriend. I stopped returning his calls, let the relationship fizzle out and graduated high school.

Soon after graduation, I was partying with a girlfriend and her own coke-selling boyfriend when Mr. Smooth Talker showed up.

"Come on, Freda. Give me another chance. I've changed," he said. "We can be together and I can be a real father for Darion. You'll see, I'll be a real family man."

His words were like cool water on my lips parched for love and I couldn't resist his offer.

Chris didn't work and didn't support me although we continued our insane on and off cycle. He moved in and out of my mother's home, was gone all night and slept all day. Strange people came to visit him. Some had sleepy eyes and stretched their slow words like taffy. Others talked too much, too fast, and bounced their restless knees as they tried to sit still on my sofa.

Once, I answered the phone to be greeted by a low, serious voice.

"Lemme talk to Chris," he said.

"He's not here. Who is this?"

"Don't you know?! He owes me a lot of money. As soon as you see him, you tell him I'm looking for him and he better have my money!"

I hadn't touched drugs while I was pregnant, but somehow, here I was, baby-mama to a drug dealer.

Clearly, I couldn't trust him with drugs or women. I rummaged through the pockets of his jeans that lay on the floor for me to wash. I dug through his backpack to find a handful of tightly creased notes. I unfolded one, bracing myself for another punch in the face.

"... I can't stop thinking about you. Last night was so special. Chris, I love you. I know you're doing the right thing, taking care of your family, but I will wait for you. Forever and Always, Erin."

Another love-thirsty girl was drowning in his lies. And at 18, I was pregnant with our second child.

Not again, I thought. *Okay, well, we can make this work. He'll marry me now because we have two kids.*

I had quit crack and Chris moved back in with my family and me. We both got jobs at McDonald's in Gap, working opposite shifts to care for Darion. And, as always, my hope died fast.

Just after our son, DeShawn, was born, Chris whined about his job and quit. "I work all day, then I'm stuck here with the kids all night," he said. "I can't go out with my friends and it's just not fair."

Not fair? His decision forced me to quit and receive public assistance because I didn't have childcare. Now *that* wasn't fair.

Chris stole money from me, spending every penny I had to provide for our boys. Our fights escalated and he would pin me to the bed with his body and scream at me nose-to-nose.

"I'm *not* doing drugs woman! You hear?! I don't want to hear any more of your sh** about me doing drugs! It's lies ...," he went on and on until his rage was satisfied.

When I was 19, I caught him cheating again and threw him out for good. It was an ugly break-up and he even called the cops to get his belongings from my house.

After a year on welfare, I was required to join a one-year job-training program where I learned Microsoft programs and secretarial work. My teacher, Linda, was impressed that I mastered each skill long before my classmates.

"I have a job opportunity for you," she said. "It would let you get credit for completing the program and get you out of here."

I was excited to take the secretarial position at Linda's accountant's office where I answered phones and compiled tax reports. I learned every new task that I could on the job and eventually was promoted to a bookkeeper position, handling accounts for six of the West Chester firm's clients.

For two years, I stayed away from drugs and men and focused on motherhood. I got lonely though and started joining friends for an occasional drink at the bar. In no time, I was coming home at six o'clock in the morning, sloshed, and even dating another liar for a while.

One day, I traded my heels for sneakers and went for my usual lunch hour walk around West Chester. As I approach the corner, I saw an old friend from high school and jogged across the street to catch him.

"Hey, Juddy!" I waved. That was his nickname in school, but his name was Justin.

"Hey, Freda. How you doin'?" he asked. After as much catching up as we could do in a few minutes, he asked for my phone number and permission to call me when I finished work.

"Sure, here you go," I dug for paper and pen in my purse. "I get done at five."

At 5:00 on the dot, my cell phone rang. We talked for my entire 45-minute drive home to Parkesburg. He was polite and respectful and told me he'd like to get together and talk some more. I wasn't sure how I felt about that because I knew he had just been released from state prison for a crime related to his former heroin addiction.

I was curious, though, and he was so handsome and spoke kindly to me. Our 5 p.m. phone calls became a daily habit that quenched my thirst for affection. He was the first man who was actually interested in *me.*

"How was your day?" was the first thing he asked. "How are the kids? What were they up to today?" He actively listened, got excited for the things that excited me and encouraged me after a bad day or challenge with the kids. We added a second daily phone date to our routine, each night after the boys were in bed.

Justin and I planned our first date to see a movie. I'd been in many relationships and so this felt like my first real date! As I drove us to the theatre, a deer darted in front of my car and I floored the brakes, but it was too late. My car had to be towed and we missed the movie.

Always one to make the best of a bad situation, Justin suggested we go to Kentucky Fried Chicken instead. He asked me all about my life and I wondered, *Could this be the guy? Or am I just fooling myself again?* In spite of his rough past, I sensed something different than all the men before. Deep down inside, Justin was good. I felt safe with him.

Justin lived with his mother in Paradise and got a job working with mill framing at Stock Building Supply. We saw each other every day and he was eager to cheer for Darion, 7, and DeShawn, 4, at their ballgames. He was quickly a welcome and consistent male presence the boys enjoyed.

Meanwhile, Chris was in and out of their lives, either spoiling them or ignoring them and almost never paying child support.

I got my own apartment for the first time in Christiana and Justin was excited to help me set up house. He bought my pots and pans and my vacuum. He helped me move my stuff in and organize it with care. Justin was all about what he could give, not what he could get from me.

Our relationship was going strong for a full year when we started to talk about marriage. With our pasts against us, we knew we needed more than each other to make it last.

"Maybe we should try going to church," I suggested.

"Yeah, I went to church when I was young," he said. "I've been thinking we should go."

I couldn't shake the sense that God wanted us to belong to a church again, but I was convinced that people there would reject me like every man in my life had until now. I was everything a Christian would disdain: an unwed mother of two who used to smoke crack and was sleeping with her ex-con boyfriend.

I pressed through my fears as we visited several churches Justin's relatives attended. Somehow, we never felt at home and I asked Justin if we could try the church of my childhood.

On its website, I learned that Victory Chapel was now called Freedom Life Christian Center. They had hired a new lead pastor just a few months earlier.

When we walked into the church foyer with my boys, someone recognized me and came running up with a hug. "Oh, my gosh! It's great to see you, Freda! How are you?" she asked.

"I'm good. This is my boyfriend, Justin," I said a little nervously. "And these are my boys, Darion and DeShawn."

"Wow! So cute!"

Others who taught me in Sunday school were excited to see me, too. There were no cold shoulders, no whispers or disapproving stares. Nothing but a warm, "Welcome home!"

Justin and I settled into a maroon cushioned pew in the middle of the sanctuary after checking the boys into children's church downstairs. We rose with the congregation when the worship band began to play.

Tears wet my cheeks from the first song. I could almost *see* the Jesus of my childhood wrap his arms around me and pull me close. My soul was quenched by an intense sensation that I was loved. God had never left me. He'd been waiting for me to come back to him and bask in his devotion.

Starting with my Dad, and then with every male rejection, I blamed God for leaving me alone and unloved. I also thought he wouldn't accept me until I cleaned myself up, which I couldn't do no matter how hard I had tried. But all along, God was waiting for me with arms open wide to come to him so he could clean me up with his love.

God really was my Daddy.

Pastor Sam shared a message and ended by asking everyone to close our eyes.

"You are not here by accident," he said. "You are here by divine appointment. God loves you and wants to forgive you of your past and give you hope and a future. He can make you into a new person today if you put your trust in Jesus. Raise your hand if you'd like to do that right now."

My hand shot up and, without looking, I knew Justin's did too. Pastor Sam led the church in prayer as my heart cried out.

Jesus, forgive me. Make me a new person. Help me follow you all the days of my life and never doubt your love again.

"If you raised your hand and prayed with us, I invite you to join us down front here so we can pray with you and encourage you."

Justin made his way out of the pew with me on his heels. Crying, we walked decisive steps to the edge of the stage. I wanted to fall on my knees and put my face in the carpet but I didn't see anyone else kneeling. Several people came to pray for Justin and me.

Afterward, we sat in the church café having donuts with the boys. Pastor Sam and Chad, the worship pastor, came right over to meet us and invite us to be a part of the church.

On the ride home, the boys couldn't stop chattering about their experience in children's church. They begged us to go back.

"This is where we need to be," Justin said. "We decided to let God put our past in the past and now we have to let him help us get our lives right."

"Definitely," I agreed.

That meant we needed to stop sleeping together until we got married. And we would certainly need God's help with that. When you've never gone there with someone, it's easier not to do it in the first place. But once you've done it, you can't back off.

"Okay, you're not spending any more nights here, Justin," I said. It was a struggle that we lost once in a while, but in the moments when we asked for God's help to resist temptation, he came through every time.

After a Christmas Eve visit at my mom's house, Justin walked the boys and me into my apartment where rose petals were scattered on the floor.

"What's this?" I asked as Darion and DeShawn choked back giggles.

"You'll see," Justin smiled.

We left the boys in the living room and followed the soft red petal path to the bedroom where Justin shut the door behind us. The trail ended in a circle on the floor.

He motioned for me to kneel with him in the circle and he picked up a ring from the floor with one hand and held my hand with the other. Slipping it onto my finger he asked, "Freda, will you marry me?"

"Yes!" This moment was better than I'd ever dreamed. This man was better than any I'd ever wanted. And we were going to make it because Jesus was in the house.

We were looking for a house to buy and money was tight so we couldn't afford a wedding just yet. I wanted to go to the Justice of the Peace to legalize our relationship, but Justin thought it would be nice for our mothers if we had a ceremony.

We tried so hard to remain abstinent, but we let our guard down a few times. In August, I learned I was pregnant and we still had not set a wedding date.

All at once we were trying to make settlement on a home, go to prenatal care, work full time and plan a hurried wedding with no money. Justin also lost his brother in a car accident during that time.

As Christmas approached, I started to show and worried what people at church were thinking of me. One day, Pastor Sam came up to us and said, "I really want to marry you guys."

"We really want to get married," we said.

Pastor Sam could have been condescending, but instead he was encouraging and helpful. He and his wife, Michele, planned the music and the flowers because I had no idea what I wanted. A church member catered the reception for free.

I carried a single white lily down the aisle wearing a white prom gown, shawl, white heels and borrowed jewelry. Step-by-slow-step, I walked the aisle to meet Justin in his black suit, pink shirt, pink tie and bright smile. Overwhelmed with love from Jesus, Justin and our new church family, I fought to keep tears from disturbing my makeup.

We moved into our home in April 2004 and our son, T.I., was born in the same month. Our daughter, Mia, completed our family in 2008.

I've been privileged to work as Freedom Life Christian Center's church administrator since 2007.

Jesus' love overwhelms me every day as I sense his presence with me. I talk to him daily and invite him to guide me through each day. His love never runs out and he never turns me away.

I'm not alone anymore. God has given me an incredible husband, wonderful children and a church family. God is the head of our home, and the center of my life. With arms open wide, he's become my daddy and so much more.

All In

Jason Rising's Back Story

Another spit wad hit me on the back of the neck as I struggled to fill in the blanks on my third grade spelling ditto. Nothing on the paper made sense, no matter how hard I tried to read it. Asking my teacher for help again would be embarrassing and, besides, she'd given up on me.

"Jason is a stupid-head," a classmate whispered at just the right volume for my ears but not the teacher's. Kids at nearby desks tried to stifle giggles.

"Yeah, he goes to the resource room because he's a retard," he continued in the wake of the increased attention.

I was a head taller than any of them and already built like a linebacker. But I was still a quiet kid at heart, so my peers in East Longmeadow, Massachusetts, didn't have anything to worry about — at least most of the time.

But on days like this one, I'd had enough of the bullying, enough name-calling, enough rejection by teachers and classmates, enough straining for correct answers and enough of being the last kid picked for kickball. My rage boiled over and this kid was going to get romped!

The bell rang and chairs scraped the tile floor as we shoved off from our desks and scrambled out the door for recess. As we filed outside, I put my arm around my antagonist's shoulder.

"Hey, buddy," I said. He looked up at me, puzzled, as I led him just a few more steps into a mud puddle. With one quick jerk, I flipped him backward into the muck and wailed on him. He may have bested me in the classroom, but not in the schoolyard!

With every rejection and every wrong answer, my anger would swell for years to come.

I was born in 1973 and as far back as kindergarten I felt the sting of rejection from both peers and adults. One of my earliest memories is playing a caged lion in the school play that year. It was the tiniest, one-second part — the most insignificant role for the most insignificant kid.

As I moved through elementary school, I took note that teachers readily helped other students with their work, but put me off. "That's just typical," they'd say when I struggled. Ultimately, they pawned me off on the resource room for one-on-one tutoring for a good part of the day. Truth was, though I struggled to learn, I wasn't stupid. I was well aware of what they thought of me.

I often wanted to give up on myself too. Any correct answer or passing grade was a formidable accomplishment, but I couldn't string many together in a row. I was so frustrated, with no way to release it!

Maybe they're right. I am just a big dummy and there's no use in trying, I sometimes thought.

I couldn't compete academically, but I could get even physically. It seemed like I was always in trouble for fighting but even when I didn't *want* to hurt people, I did. I was an awkward giant, accidentally overpowering kids while wrestling, playing football or just horsing around the house. Big Mean Stupid Jason was always in trouble for something and each reprimand fermented my insecurity and rage.

In fourth grade, there were a couple of teachers in the resource room who were kind and patient with me. But I was prone to fits of kicking and screaming in frustration too wild even for them. During these episodes they sent me to the janitor's closet in desperation. The short, dark-haired man with little glasses and blue coveralls never said much, but always listened thoughtfully to my chatter. It was possibly the only place outside of home that I felt accepted. He would let me mop floors for a while — not as punishment, but a Hail Mary pass to help me settle down.

It was the early 1980s and even those few adults who hadn't written me off were desperate to know what to do with me.

"We have one more thing we can try," the elementary guidance counselor told my mother. "There's this new experimental drug you could ask your pediatrician about that's supposed to help kids like Jason. It's called Ritalin."

Mom's response, as always, was to pray.

Mom was Catholic and when I was about 6 or 7 she decided to give religion more than lip service and rote rituals. She wanted to learn as much as she could about Jesus and she wanted me to know him too.

She told me all about him and we kneeled together at her bedside in front of a formal rendering of Jesus. This robed Messiah had blue eyes, fair skin and a halo disk behind his head while his hand was lifted ever so slightly as if in blessing or instruction. Mom guided me to ask Jesus to help me know him, too, and I did so sincerely.

I even served as an altar boy until our priest directed Mom to a Baptist church as a more suitable place for her fervent spiritual quest.

Dad didn't buy into this uncharted territory called Ritalin and Mom was convinced I had some sort of brain damage and God would heal me. No school official was going to sway my kind, but tenacious parents any differently. Not even in fourth grade, when they were advised to yank me from school for good and teach me a trade.

"Something he can do with his hands," they said. "He could be a good painter, or maybe learn construction."

By that point, I had given up on myself, too. I maxed out on effort, but no matter how hard I tried, the letters seemed mixed up on the page and I just couldn't focus enough to retain what the teachers told me. *I'm dumb as sticks,* I told myself. *Why should I try anymore?*

Mom and Dad saw I was losing heart and although the public school gave up on me, they weren't about to do the same. They enrolled me in a small, private Christian school in Springfield, Massachusetts.

Dad had just left his career as a ShopRite meat cutter to start his own commercial cleaning business when they sent me to private school. We had a modest home in the suburbs and always had food on the table, but paying for school was no easy feat.

Classrooms were small with 6–10 students. I got a lot of individual attention from people who, like my mother, just *knew* God would heal my affliction.

Over the next few years, I steadily improved. Like the *Little Engine That Could*, I pushed up the steep mountain to learn.

I have two sisters; Natalie, is 3 or 4 years older than me and Jennifer, who is about 2 years younger than me. I got along well with both of them, but hung out with Jennifer the most because we were closer in age.

Our house and two others were on a dirt road, which began off the cul de sac of a more traditional development. My cousin lived just through the woods, and there was another boy who my sisters, cousin and I hung out with. We played ball, wrestled, explored the woods, rode bikes and watched sports.

Mr. Sanders was a retired widower in the neighborhood that sometimes invited all of us kids over when we were running around the neighborhood. He would also keep an eye on us if our parents had to run a quick errand sometimes. One day, when I was about 10, I was there by myself. He sat down next to me and opened a magazine.

"Look at this," he said, turning the pages with images no child should see. Then his wrinkled old hands touched me in ways a child should never be touched. This happened several times over the next two years. I hated it! It was one more thing to bloat my anger and I could never seem to get the words out to tell my parents.

One day when I was 12, I was lying on the floor petting my part-Chihuahua, Sparky, as he ate from his bowl.

"Okay, Jason, you're going to go over to Mr. Sanders' for a bit while Mom and I run a couple of errands," Dad said.

"No. I'm not going over there," I said, continuing to watch Sparky eat.

Surprised by my directness, Mom asked, "Why not?"

"He touched me," I said. *There. It's out.*

My parents tried to be calm for my sake, explaining that nothing was my fault — that Mr. Sanders is a dirty old man and I never had to go there again. Later, I learned Dad wanted to march over and "kill" him, but Mom took more of a "forgive and move on" approach which led to quite a few disagreements when I wasn't present. I don't blame them for not retaliating or calling the police because it wasn't something people talked about or reported back then.

Mom coaxed me to talk to her often about what happened which was therapeutic. After each of our conversations, she would sit next to me, place her hands on my head and pray out loud that God would heal my hurt and anger.

One summer, probably after fifth grade, some neighborhood kids and I started stealing Camels from a corner store. We'd split four packs and smoke them in the woods in one day.

I stole other small things from stores and slashed a few tires. A couple of us even broke into someone's house hoping to find keys to their '87 Toyota Supra and take a joy ride. Thank God we didn't find the keys!

Dad and Mom never knew about my mischief, but all the while, Mom prayed.

Dad always had time for me and we usually spent it playing sports or watching movies like *The Magnificent Seven* and *The Great Escape*.

"Hey, Jason, look what I brought home," Dad called out when he got home from work.

"What?" I asked, my big feet thumping down the stairs in a hurry to greet him.

Hockey sticks!

We scrounged up a tennis ball and went straight to my bedroom where we knocked it around on the hardwood floor using the baseboard as our goal. We roughhoused with our sticks so often that the baseboard got pretty beat up.

Dad was a hard-working man who often came home physically and mentally exhausted. But all those years, no matter how weary or stressed he was, he spent a good hour playing with me after work.

Like most kids, when I was real young I couldn't throw a ball to save my life. I'd launch that pigskin with all my might sending it flailing right over Dad's head!

"It's okay, buddy, no problem," he'd say.

He would chase the ball and return to his position, only for me to overthrow it again. And again. And again. It didn't matter how many times he chased that ball, he never once complained.

Dad would also look me in the eye and say, "I love you" just often enough that I knew he really meant it. To this day, he is my hero.

Dad was almost always in the stands or on the sidelines when I played sports for the township league. I tried baseball, but it was too boring for me. In fact, one time I took off my glove and just sat down in the outfield to watch ants in the dirt! But football and soccer were a different story. By junior high, I'd grown out of my two left feet and learned to control my hulking body. On the field, my brawn and intensity finally found a home.

I played center full, fullback and right half in soccer. My average skill was boosted by my tenacity to play with all my might. I was passionate about sports and playing gave me an appropriate place to expel my physical energy.

In football, I excelled at both offense and defense so much so that the school district scouted me and begged my mom to put me in public high school.

"No way," Mom dug in her heals. "He's so good at football that he will get lost again academically and start drinking beer and having sex and all that football star stuff."

There is no doubt in my mind that she was right.

I was disappointed though. I loved everything about the gridiron, especially hitting people with all my pent up anger and not getting in trouble for it! Once I knocked a kid out cold on the line in practice. When I played defense, our opposition triple teamed me to keep me from sacking the quarterback. Sports — particularly football — were the only place I could go all out physically and be applauded.

I played soccer for my Christian high school. In the fall of my junior year, we won three straight matches to enter the playoffs as the last seed. Then we beat the team that held the league championship for years. We bested a few more teams and found ourselves in the final match.

The score was 1–1 and I was on defense. We were on the defensive end and I set the ball just outside the line, parallel to the goal, for a corner kick. A few quick steps forward and I kicked my signature curve ball into the goal! They called it back because the ball had to be in play first. But it was the coolest shot!

We scored again and held our opponents off for the rest of the match. When the seconds ticked down, the ref blew the final whistle. We'd won! We ran toward each other, jumping wildly, sharing high-fives and corralling together.

"This is so God!" A friend of mine exclaimed.

"What are you talking about? God had nothing to do with it," I quipped. As I had entered my teens, I put Mom's God on the sidelines, so much so that I doubted his existence. As far as I was concerned, any victory in the classroom or on the field was the fruit of my tenacity, not God's providence.

"This is God, man! He won this huge game."

"No, *we* won this game. There is no God," I insisted.

"Victory lap!" someone shouted.

We ran down the sideline, turned the first corner, and as we turned the second corner, collapsed collectively from exhaustion. We'd given everything that day and pushed ourselves to the edge.

Several of us earned spots on the All-Star team, which won two years in a row.

I was angry and mischievous, but still, Dad spent quality time with me and Mom never stopped praying that God would intervene in my life.

"Huh?" I stirred out of a deep sleep to find Mom standing over me, her olive oil-soaked fingertip on my forehead.

"Father, you said this in Isaiah 61:1 and I ask it for my son," she whispered, then quoted the Bible verse from memory. "'The Spirit of the Sovereign Lord is upon me, for the Lord has anointed me to preach good news to the poor. He has sent me to comfort the broken-hearted and to proclaim that captives will be released and prisoners will be freed from darkness.' Jesus, please comfort Jason's broken heart and free him from darkness, then use him to do the same for others."

"Mom, get away. Go back to bed," I pushed her hand away and rolled over.

So that's why I have zits in the middle of my forehead and yellow stains on my pillowcase and white doorframe!

She did this almost every night, sometimes as late as 2 a.m. Sometimes, I woke up; sometimes, I didn't.

Mom's oil-ridden prayers must have worked because by my grades improved steadily through high school. I even made honor roll junior year! My confidence grew and in junior high and high school I made some good friends. I wasn't picked on anymore.

When I was younger, our family plugged in to the Baptist church and grew strong roots there. But after some years, Mom grew restless and led us to an Assemblies of God church, and soon after to a nondenominational church.

Dad and I didn't care for this hyper-charismatic group that today I would consider cultish. He quit church altogether, and I was disillusioned to watch many men and families fall away from God because of their experiences at that church.

But Mom insisted my sisters and me join her there. We hated it, but didn't push back much because we respected her wishes. If Mom wanted us to do something, that was that.

In spite of academic improvement and a physical outlet on the field, the anger I seemed to be born with expanded in my teen years. By 16, I hated everything, especially religion, church and anything to do with God.

By the time I was 17, Mom left Crazy Church for an Assemblies of God church several towns over from where we lived.

The youth pastor took me to McDonald's for lunch every couple of weeks where I did nothing but gripe and cuss about God and church.

"I hate your stinkin' youth group," I said. "It's stupid and I hate the people there. Besides, I'm not a good person. You shouldn't want me there."

"Well, I hear you. But just know that we don't hate you. We love you and so does God," he responded calmly. Unoffended, he would invite me to lunch again.

I brimmed with so much anger that it seemed to seep out my pores to escape. Verbal and physical fights were my norm again. From sophomore year on, my attitude had been *screw you, I'll do whatever I want.*

I worked as a nursing home dietary aide throughout high school. One day, I grabbed a pack of wine coolers and five cold Budweiser's we stored for one of the old men. I got together with another kid from school and we tried it out. I hated the beer, but downed half of it simply because it was forbidden fruit. I finished all the wine coolers though and got really buzzed.

Yeah, this isn't attractive to me, I thought. It was the first and last time I ever drank.

My anger turned inward and by January of junior year, I was depressed. Friday nights I sat staring out the window at home with a stomachache. *I just want to die,* I thought, though I never considered suicide.

This girl who had probably banged most of the guys at school said, "I know what will cheer you up. We should have sex."

"I've never done that before," I said, curious. I'd had plenty of girlfriends though. And she wasn't one of them.

"Well, we should. Trust me, I'll make you happy," she said.

Why she slept with so many guys, I'll never know. But I didn't mind being next in line. "Yeah, okay. When I get back from camp," I agreed.

Mom had mandated I go on the winter retreat in Pittsfield with my youth group that weekend. I would definitely rather sneak off with this girl than go to camp.

"I don't feel like going, and besides, it's stupid," I argued. But my push back stopped there. My parents had paid for me to go and I respected them too much to dig in my heels.

I rode one of the buses that delivered most of our 80-plus kids from youth group to the rustic camp a few hours from home. Gray smoke drifted from the chimneys of the 1950s facility while fireplaces warmed the cabin-style building. A rustic mountain chapel stood on the hilltop.

We had game time in a cozy room with the fire roaring. I played Risk on a boxy MacIntosh computer with a square keyboard. I played with Bob, a youth leader and keyboard musician on the worship team. Like our youth pastor, he took an interest in me and had been teaching me to play keys.

Each night we had chapel services where we'd sing along with the worship band and hear an energetic sermon from the youth pastor. That first evening, January 19, 1991, I shuffled into the chapel and sat in the back to quietly do my time for Mom.

"As the deer panteth for the water so my soul longeth after thee," we stood to sing the slow, but still popular 1981 melody. "You alone are my heart's desire and I long to worship thee."

Some people lifted their hands and gently swayed, eyes closed. I gripped the back of the outdated wooden pew with both hands and let my mind wander from this foolishness. I came to suddenly during the next, more upbeat song and looked down to see myself clapping to the beat like everyone else.

What am I doing? I thought.

Then some inner, urgent impulse took over. *I gotta go up front. I'm saved, but I don't care, I've gotta get saved again. God is so real!*

Without invitation, as the student congregation sang, I ran down the center aisle to the front of the stage. I fell to my knees with my face in my hands and sobbed. I hadn't cried since childhood.

I've been so angry, God. So angry. And I've done so much bad stuff, my heart cried out. *Take it. Take it all away. I don't want to be like this anymore. Take my life. Change me. If anyone can change me, it's you!*

Singing continued and as I confessed my desperation for a fresh start, I was vaguely aware of a few whispers in the front pew behind me. My youth pastor was on the stage leading the songs and when I finally looked up, my eyes caught his confused expression. Even after all the faith he'd had in me, he was shocked to watch me purge my heart to God.

My body shook with my sobs — deep heaving sobs, like a father who's lost a son. I tried unsuccessfully to hold back the tide of snot and phlegm that oozed from my nostrils and throat.

A peaceful, yet sobering heaviness that none could deny settled in the room and my ears caught more whispers.

"I can't believe *Jason Rising* is at the altar," some said.

"God is here," observed others reverently.

God is real. Jesus is real. He's here. He loves me, the revelation exploded in my heart and mind. *I'm not insignificant! God has a purpose for my life.*

I kneeled there, humbled, while my youth pastor continued to lead the band.

And then they came. As the first few students left the pews to join me, others followed to crowd the altar, sobbing in contrition. It seemed like just 10 minutes passed, but four hours after rushing the altar, I got up from my knees. It was midnight.

I climbed the stage and took the mic from my youth pastor. "Jesus is real, you guys! He's so real and you have to serve him. He loves you. Give your life to him, now!" I pleaded with tears and a quivering lip.

"And come up here. All of you should come up here and give this pastor a hug," I said, putting my arm around his shoulders. "He's the best d*** youth pastor," my voice broke as I wept and wiped my eyes. The raw expression was actually an improvement over my usual foul language — a habit God helped me break soon afterward.

Without hesitation, my peers lined up and paraded across the stage to hug the man I once disdained.

Mine was the first, but not the only life given away to Jesus that night. Tens of others wept before God, too. We were all in.

Mom met me at church when the buses arrived. I didn't have to say a word. One look at me and she knew her prayers had been answered. A few days later, my parents called me into the living room.

"Here, we have something for you," Mom said, handing me a Bible. I opened the cover and read familiar handwriting on the gift dedication page.

"Jason Matthew Rising, Love, Mom and Dad, January 24, 1991."

I read that Bible every day. (I still do.) I wanted to know all I could about Jesus and live out the plan he had for my life.

From that point forward, I was in church every time the doors were open. At youth group, ten of us who went all in with Jesus at camp sat with open Bibles in the front row, eagerly taking notes on the lesson. I quickly abandoned my plans with the loose girl from school.

Within two years, I had gone on mission trips to Mexico and Texas, preached my first sermon at youth group and preached on the street in Springfield, Massachusetts.

Jesus transformed me that snotty night at camp. My parents knew it. My youth pastor knew it. My teachers knew it. Everybody knew it. I wasn't the same angry, rebellious Jason anymore. I knew I was loved and I knew my purpose was to share God's love with others.

Jesus, please comfort Jason's broken heart and free him from darkness, then use him to do the same for others.

God had answered a mother's tenacious, midnight prayers. And he wasn't done yet.

I had a knack for creating human videos — inspirational mini dramas pantomimed to popular Christian music. I would share all kinds of crazy ideas with my youth pastor to get kids to come to youth group and hear about God's love and freedom.

"How about we have a luau in January? We can pump the heat to like 90 degrees in the gymnasium, decorate it with tropical stuff, have Hawaiian food and wear Hawaiian shirts and leis," I said enthusiastically.

He let me run with it and it became an annual event. After I'd moved on, I found out that every year five or six churches were involved with it and several hundred kids attended. But the best part was that many were experiencing Jesus like I did on Snot Day at camp!

On the mission trip to Mexico I sensed that God was calling me to ministry. I called home to tell my mom.

"We've been just serving people here, Mom, and telling them about Jesus," I said. "This is what I want to do with my life."

"Where?" she asked.

"Well, I don't think it's in a foreign place. I think I'm supposed to be an evangelist, but I'm just not sure yet."

"Yeah, I've always known that."

Of course she did.

The Spirit of the Sovereign Lord is upon me, for the Lord has anointed me to preach good news to the poor.

I graduated in 1991 and spent a year working and saving for college. I started at Central Bible College in Springfield, Missouri in 1992.

The process was gradual, but God had surely rewarded Mom's pleas to heal my mind in order for me to make it this far. And he did it in high school while I was still angry and rejecting him! If only the teachers and schools who wrote me off could see where God had brought me!

Still, my pull to evangelism wasn't clear. The only thing I was sure of was that I wouldn't be a suit-and-tie guy that traveled from church to church. But where would I fit?

Kathy, my girlfriend since 11th grade, also went to CBC. I gave her a one-karat diamond and proposed. Life was really coming together for me.

Kathy stayed at CBC and I transferred to Valley Forge Christian College in Phoenixville, Pennsylvania, for my sophomore year.

I still had no clarity about what "evangelism" would look like for me, but was confident of my call to it. Maybe a little too confident.

On the first day of school, I stepped into the registration line, briefcase in hand.

"Hi, how are you? My name is Teri. I'm a senior, what year are you?" said a friendly brunette with the warmest smile.

I was all business.

"Hi," I stood up straight and confident, as if I wasn't tall enough. "I'm Jason Rising. I'm going to be an evangelist," I said, shaking her hand as if greeting a pastor for a potential invitation to speak.

We would become casual acquaintances with mutual friends and later laughed at my misplaced professionalism.

Meanwhile, Kathy and I planned to meet at home in Massachusetts over Christmas break.

"C'mon Kathy, I'm getting worried. Please call me back," I left yet another phone message during semester finals. We'd been bickering off and on, but nothing could be *that* wrong, could it?

On my drive home through Connecticut, I called again from a truck stop payphone. Not recognizing the number on the Caller I.D., Kathy's mother answered.

"Hello."

"Hi this is Jason. Is Kathy there?"

She hesitated and sniffled. She'd started to cry and handed the phone to her daughter.

"Stop calling! I hate you!" Kathy blindsided me. I got an earful of how terrible I was until she screamed, "… and I don't ever want to see you again!" Then she hung up on me.

Hot, wet coals pooled in my eyes and I kept them from spilling just long enough to get to my car. I shut the door, dropped my head to the steering wheel and broke. I banged on the dash and sobbed almost as hard as I did at camp until I could pull it together enough to drive.

When I got home, Kathy was waiting to give me the ring and pick up her stuff. She drove away and it was the last I ever saw her.

I fasted for three days over Christmas break, consuming only water and bread. I wanted to spend more time in prayer, so when I returned to Valley Forge I dropped my credit hours from 18 to 13 and cut my work schedule from 25 hours a week to 10–12 hours for the semester.

As heartbroken as I was, I couldn't shake the feeling that God was in control and about to do something big in my life.

Instead of going home for the summer, I joined a team doing street preaching and outreaches in Philadelphia.

After a hot dog cookout one warm night in May, streetlights cast a soft yellow glow on the asphalt of the vacant lot next to a crack house in the Frankfurt projects. At about 11:00, I performed a solo human video then invited people to pray with me for freedom through Jesus. Many came forward to yield themselves to God's love, just as I had done at youth camp.

As I looked over almost 100 people crowding the lot and spilling into the street, my fuzzy call to evangelism started to come into focus.

Holy Hands.

Creative, relevant, blue jeans and t-shirt presentations of Truth that would change lives like Jesus changed mine. And, just like I'd done in sports, I would run fast and hit hard. I'd go big or go home.

The following summer, in 1996, I launched the first Holy Hands tour. I recruited fellow Valley Forge students to do ministry similar to what I'd done the previous summer.

Teri — my friend from the registration line — had graduated and worked as a secretary on campus while she figured out her next steps in ministry. She had applied for a job with internationally known evangelist, Ron Luce. He had prayed with her about it, but hadn't made an offer. In the meantime, she sensed a pull to join Holy Hands. She started asking questions about Holy Hands and my need for an assistant on the summer 1997 tour starting soon.

I was curt in our interview.

"What you're doing sounds like the kind of thing I want to be involved in," she said.

"Well, if you want to do this, you can do it. But I could care less. Just let me know soon," I said.

She had a lot of praying to do, because she couldn't stand me. I was curt. I was abrupt with her, like I would be with any guy. I wasn't trying to be rude, I was just an intense dude, 100 percent in the game God asked me to play. And after my crushing break-up with Kathy, I tuned women out for a while.

It wasn't long before Teri politely declined Ron Luce's offer and jumped on board with this fledgling evangelist. And she was all in. No reservations.

Teri's opinion of me changed on tour—so much so that on our Fourth of July break, she told her mother, "I think I'm going to marry this guy."

Soon afterwards, we were near Giant Stadium at the Meadowlands Marriot doing an inner-city ministry conference. In the lobby, Teri asked if she could talk with me and we walked to the van.

Somehow the subject of having a relationship came up.

"It's never gonna happen," I hit the issue hard.

"Okay," she said professional and expressionless.

Inside she was crushed, but she never let me see it.

As I drove our team in the van that night, I glanced in the rearview mirror to see her sleeping in one of the back seats. I was annoyed.

You admit you have feelings for me and then you act like you don't care that I turned you down?

But all the while she was aching inside, pretending to sleep. She was handling my rejection with dignity and honor while I thought she didn't care.

After that, I didn't think of her as one of the guys. I noticed her beauty and took note of her character. *Should I consider this? I'm content being single. Would it be another disaster?*

I called home to confide in my mom. "Man, I'm not sure what I should do." She advised me to keep praying and promised to do the same.

Our tour took us to Detroit where I watched Teri go about her duties. God gave me clarity in a moment. *This girl is gorgeous and amazing! I think I'm in love with her.*

I called Mom again.

"This is the girl I want to marry."

I shared my feelings with Teri and told her I'd like to date her when tour ended in a few weeks because of our policy of no dating on tour. We married the following spring, before going on tour again.

For the next nine years we did the *Holy Hands* summer tours, each one bigger and better. We brought teens and young adults on board as summer interns and they helped train youth group teams to do ministry in cities around the East Coast.

Along the way we had our sons, Joshua in 1999 and Caleb in 2002.

During non-touring months, I worked in various ministry positions over the years. I partnered with an evangelism ministry in Delaware for a while. At other times I was a meter reader, a youth pastor and a senior associate pastor. We uprooted several times, living in New Jersey, Michigan and Pennsylvania.

Life in the ministry wasn't easy. We saw ministers fall into sin or just give up. We watched church people rise up to eject a godly pastor from the pulpit. We were burned more than a few times and often didn't know where our next check was coming from. It was hard not to become jaded.

Like my school days, sometimes I wondered if I should quit. But I love people and want them to know the God who transforms lives! I couldn't give up on loving and serving them because God never gave up on me.

As with sports, I hit through the line with hard intensity and bounced up when I was sacked. But I wouldn't last to the fourth quarter by running full speed toward the goal line.

By 2004, I'd been on the senior pastoral staff of a church of several thousand for a few years. I was responsible for a large staff and many ministries, including: junior and senior high, children's ministry, college and career ministry, Holy Hands Bible Institute and Holy Hands Tour.

I worked five days a week from 6 a.m. to 9 p.m. and was never really off on my two days off. At 2 p.m. each day, I locked the door to my office, turned out the lights and slept on my floor for an hour before the next meeting.

My home life was nonexistent. When I prayed, I felt nothing. When I read my Bible, it was just words. I felt like I had lost my relationship with God.

As I roamed the aisles of the grocery store to pick up a few things, I found myself in the alcohol section, staring at shelves lined with wine bottles and wine coolers.

Why am I contemplating this? I don't do this and it's never interested me.

It happened more than once and it scared me. I thought I was losing my mind.

I resigned in May 2005 from sheer exhaustion. After three months off, I went to EMERGE Ministries in Akron, Ohio, for three days of intense evaluation and therapy. Teri came with me. After a battery of extensive tests with hundreds of questions, they gave it to me straight.

"You are suffering burnout," the counselor said.

"Yeah, I'm exhausted," I replied.

"No, you don't get it. You have burnout—a clinical condition as a result of pushing yourself to emotional limits. The good news is, with God's help we can get you well. But it will take time."

We talked about how I set myself up for this. I failed to set personal boundaries. I failed to maintain a balanced lifestyle. I failed to set up my life and ministry for longevity. I was kicking goals, but at this pace and intensity, I wouldn't complete the victory lap.

"What hobbies do you have," the counselor asked. "What do you do in your free time?"

I thought for a moment. "Nothing."

"This is where your problem is," he leaned back in his chair, and pointed at me.

"I only like ministry. I don't have anything else."

"What did you enjoy when you were a kid?"

"Sports."

"Then you make sports a priority in your life."

I started reading the sports page and watching ESPN. I followed the Red Sox and started collecting memorabilia. I go to a game at least once a year no matter the cost. It's more than a day at the ballpark — it's an investment in my well-being.

I continued counseling for several months back home and I traveled, speaking in churches and coaching pastors and leaders. We bought a house a mile from Teri's parents in New Castle, Pennsylvania. It was refreshing to be somewhere that I wasn't known as "Jason Rising. Evangelist," like my first words to Teri. I was simply Jason Rising, husband, father and neighbor cutting his lawn.

I still tend to go all in, but Teri knows when to throw a flag on the play and I know not to challenge her call. She'll pull me aside and say, "We're taking a break. It's time for you to unplug."

It's been amazing to watch how regular timeouts have helped my game. I burned out trying to answer God's call with complete abandon. The problem was, I relied on my own strength and priorities, not his.

Today, I coach leaders at my new home church, Freedom Life Christian Center. With the help of God, Teri and an incredible staff, we continue to run our evangelism ministry called First Fruits.

Within First Fruits, there are three ministries and more to come within the next five years. One is Holy Hands, which continues to develop young adults to coach teens in sharing God's love.

The Spirit of the Sovereign Lord is upon me, for the Lord has anointed me to preach good news to the poor.

Garbonics creates multimedia storytelling productions using drama, STOMP, human video, dance, video and more. And Push Back is our three-day interactive conference for local churches to teach Christians how to bring hope to their communities.

He has sent me to comfort the broken-hearted and to proclaim that captives will be released and prisoners will be freed from darkness.

First Fruits will expand in the next few years with Holy Hands Bible Institute to train young people for the ministry. And Young 501 will help young adults set up nonprofit organizations that reach out to those who need to know God's love.

In Scranton one night, during the most recent Holy Hands tour, Teri and I reflected on our journey as our boys slept soundly on an air mattress next to us.

"Remember this intern and that intern," She said, naming them.

"Yeah. They're both youth pastors now," I said. "And you know so-and-so, she's a missionary now, and that other kid is doing youth evangelism."

We cried tears of gratitude as we counted off more than a decade of Holy Hands interns. Many are pastors, youth pastors, evangelists and missionaries. Others display Jesus' love in secular vocations and are "all in" as leaders in their local churches. Jesus rocked my world at youth camp, and has let me be a part of his plan to transform lives ever since.

Jesus, please comfort Jason's broken heart and free him from darkness, then use him to do the same for others.

And that's exactly what he's done.

Conclusion

I love stories. I must confess that my favorite stories are ones with happy endings. I love stories that are full of struggle, intrigue, mystery, romance and rescue. That's why I love God's story so much — that epic love story that we call the Bible. Within its pages are the stories of people who found themselves in difficult chapters of their lives where all hope seemed lost. Much like me, I'm sure you've found yourself in that place before as well! Hopelessness, brokenness, sin and despair were all part of my back story, too. In fact, my back story would *be* my story if it wasn't for Jesus.

No matter what chapter of life you find yourself in today, my greatest desire is for you to know that God has already written a happy ending for you! The Bible — God's love story — tells us that he has a hope and a future for you and me! (Jeremiah 29:11) Please know that "... God loved the world so much that he gave his one and only Son, so that everyone who believes in him will not perish but have eternal life." (John 3:16, NLT) You and I are living in God's story right now — the story of our rescue from ourselves, from our sin and from our own failure. (Romans 3:23; 6:23)

I don't need to convince you of the reality of your sin, mistakes and wrong choices. Each and every one of us has a God-sized hole in our hearts that cannot be satisfied with the things of this world in which we live. Each of us has missed the mark and has lived under the weight of those choices. Are you in that place right now, in need of God to write a new story in your life? If so, the Bible tells us that "... Everyone who calls on the name of the LORD will be saved." (Romans 10:13, NLT)

God desires to meet you right where you are, right now, and write a happy ending to your life story! He really does have a hope and a future for you!

For prayer or for more information about how to begin a relationship with God, email us at hope@freedomlife.tv.

Sam Masteller
Lead Pastor
Freedom Life Christian Center

We welcome you to visit us at:

Freedom Life Christian Center
P.O. Box 10
447 Noble Road
Christiana, PA 17509

(610) 593-5959

www.freedomlife.tv

www.mybackstory.tv